Head Covering

A FORGOTTEN **CHRISTIAN** PRACTICE
FOR **MODERN** TIMES

Jeremy Gardiner has written a thoughtful and helpful argument from Scripture and church history for women to cover their heads in worship. This book deserves a fair hearing from all who desire to obey God's Word in whatever it teaches.

-**Dr. Joel R. Beeke**, president of *Puritan Reformed Theological Seminary*

Jeremy Gardiner's book gently, respectfully, and accurately addresses all of the questions I had as I grappled with the passage in 1 Corinthians 11 on head covering. I appreciate his careful and thorough exegesis of the passage and his willingness to tackle all of the current objections and alternate views on the subject. He stays true to sound doctrine and is reasonable in his approach of what is – for many of us – an unfamiliar topic. I wish I had this resource decades ago and would encourage any believer to read it and prayerfully consider this passage for himself/herself.

-**April Cassidy**, author of *The Peaceful Wife: Living in Submission to Christ as Lord*

The book you hold in your hands is more important than you might think. I've come to understand that this "small" issue of Christian head covering is nothing of the sort. Not only is the Church's ability to faithfully exegete the Sacred Text at stake, but as we look at culture, we also see the systematic loss of what the symbol represents. Jeremy has done a great service for the Body of Christ by helping to resurrect the LORD's commands for His own worship. May the LORD forgive us for thinking we know better.

-**Dr. Carlton C. McLeod**, senior pastor of *Calvary Revival Church Chesapeake* and founder of *D6 Reformation*

Jeremy Gardiner has done the church good service in calling us back to the obedience of God's Word our parents and grandparents rejected a century ago. Gardiner gives a clear explanation of the Scriptural command, going on to treat with accuracy and kindness the many objections moderns have raised.

-**Tim Bayly,** former executive director of *The Council on Biblical Manhood & Womanhood* and author of *Daddy Tried*

I started wearing a head covering (in a church that does not wear head coverings) a few years ago. I felt challenged to put the word of God above the word of man at every turn, and to resist relativizing its teachings according to my own culture — even my Christian culture. I commend the courage of Jeremy Gardiner in standing for the whole counsel of God.

-**Andrée Seu Peterson**, senior writer at *WORLD Magazine*

Head Covering: A Forgotten Christian Practice for Modern Times
© 2016 by Jeremy Gardiner

Published by: The Head Covering Movement
1123 – 49A Street NW
Edmonton, AB T6L 4C5
www.headcoveringmovement.com

ISBN: 978-0-9952036-0-0

Head Covering

A FORGOTTEN **CHRISTIAN** PRACTICE
FOR **MODERN** TIMES

JEREMY GARDINER

headcoveringmovement.com

Contents

A Biblical Case for Modern Head Covering

Objections to Head Covering

Practical Application

Concluding Thoughts

Appendices

An Introduction to a Neglected Doctrine

"It is noticeable, in the first place, that St. Paul regards this question [about head covering] as worth deciding, and does not brush it aside as trivial. There is a right, and a wrong way of worshipping God." [1]
H.L. Goudge, Regius Professor of Divinity,
Oxford University, 1923–38

Head covering is *not* a popular doctrine. In fact, that's quite the understatement. So why would I write a book on it? Do I enjoy controversy? Absolutely not. Looking to be divisive? The opposite. Then what would possess me to do such a thing? The short answer is, because it's in the Bible.

See, if *"all Scripture is inspired by God and profitable for teaching, for reproof, for correction, for training in righteousness"* (2 Timothy 3:16), then all Scripture deserves fair treatment. On top of that, this particular topic is not just mentioned in the Bible, it is defended. There are not only one or two obscure verses, but the topic occupies fifteen consecutive verses. We can debate what Paul meant, and we can debate how it applies in the twenty-first century, but the one thing we cannot do is ignore this topic.

Dr. Daniel B. Wallace, one of the leading textual critics and founder of the Center for the Study of New Testament Manuscripts, teaches New Testament Studies at Dallas Theological Seminary. To say this brother knows the New

---

1. H.L. Goudge, *The First Epistle to the Corinthians* (Methuen and Co. Ltd., 1926), 97.

Testament and Greek text well would be understated. He said this about the "modern head covering" view (the position I am advocating), which I think many can relate to:

"The argument that a real head covering is in view and that such is applicable today is, in some respects, the easiest view to defend exegetically and the hardest to swallow practically. Since it is never safe to abandon one's conscience regarding the truth of Scripture, I held to this view up until recently. Quite frankly, I did not like it (it is very unpopular today). But I could not, in good conscience, disregard it."[2]

That's an incredibly honest statement! Because a head covering is a visual symbol, it is impossible to hide or delay in stating your views. This is the first doctrine that people know women believe when you meet them at church, even before you shake their hands. They may feel judged just by you wearing one (because they are not), and you wonder if they think you're stuck in the fifties. To top it off, your pastors or those closest to you may be concerned that you're embracing legalism.

These are real struggles people face when even contemplating the "modern head covering" view. So, suffice it to say, when Dr. Wallace notes that the head covering is "unpopular today," he has an accurate perception of how well this practice is received. When a woman wears a head covering, it forces everyone in church to think about the topic, and some just aren't ready to or don't wish to.

Daniel Wallace also says:

"The real danger, as I see it, is that many Christians simply ignore what this text says because any form of obedience to it is inconvenient."[3]

---

2. Daniel B. Wallace, "What is the Head Covering in 1 Cor 11:2–16 and Does it Apply to Us Today?" (Bible.org, 2004) https://bible.org/article/what-head-covering-1-cor-112-16-and-does-it-apply-us-today.

3. Ibid.

Now this is not to say that the only reason people don't embrace head covering is fear. Some are persuaded by other interpretations and, if convinced by Scripture, would change their minds. I hope this is you and that you share my desire to rightly understand everything the Bible says and to submit to it. However, I am concerned that many read over 1 Corinthians 11 and think, *that can't possibly mean what I think it says. No one I know wears one, and we can't all be wrong.* Then we quickly move on to chapter 12, making a mental note to look into it later (which, if we're honest, rarely happens).

If I just described your response, now is that time. Let's go deep into the text and wrestle through it together. Don't worry, though, this book isn't written to scholars. I wrote it for the average Christian, the layman and laywoman—for you.

In the next chapter I will give you an overview of the history of Christian head covering. Then in the following six chapters, I will make a biblical case that women should wear a cloth head covering while in church. Likewise, I argue that men are commanded to keep a bare head (meaning no hats) in the same context. I will do this by pointing to five reasons the apostle Paul himself gives in 1 Corinthians 11. When I explain those reasons, I won't give as much attention to competing views since this will largely be a positive presentation. After that, we will examine some of the most popular objections and practical questions. Finally, we'll wrap it up with a personal exhortation for you to embrace this symbol, even if others do not.

The Heart of the Matter

Before this introduction comes to an end, I want to bring up a word of caution: make sure your heart is prepared. I figure most people reading this book either disagree with or don't know what to make of head coverings. So your guard is probably up. I know, I do it too, and it's not a bad thing, really. We're always in a battle against false teaching and false teachers, so it's good to be skeptical and keep a sharp eye, filtering everything through the Word of God. Just make sure you won't accept any old argument against head covering because you don't want this doctrine to be true. *What will my husband or wife think? What will those in my church think? How will I find a spouse if he/she knows I believe this?*

The fear of man can be overwhelming, but we must fear God and His commands above men. We must bind ourselves to the text of Scripture and obey, no matter how uncomfortable the outcome may be. So if your heart is not ready, make sure you stop and seek the Lord in prayer before moving on. Then, when you're ready, give 1 Corinthians 11:2–16 a good read. Please read through this text slowly and become intimately familiar with it. This is the only chapter in the Bible that commands and explains the practice of head covering, so you must know it well to be a good Berean (see Acts 17:11).

Read 1 Corinthians 11:2–16

(2) Now I praise you because you remember me in everything and hold firmly to the traditions, just as I delivered them to you. (3) But I want you to understand that Christ is the head of every man, and the man is the head of a woman, and God is the head of Christ. (4) Every man who has *something* on his head while praying or prophesying disgraces his head. (5) But every woman who has her head uncovered while praying or prophesying disgraces her head, for she is one and the same as the woman whose head is shaved. (6) For if a woman does not cover her head, let her also have her hair cut off; but if it is disgraceful for a woman to have her hair cut off or her head shaved, let her cover her head. (7) For a man ought not to have his head covered, since he is the image and glory of God; but the woman is the glory of man. (8) For man does not originate from woman, but woman from man; (9) for indeed man was not created for the woman's sake, but woman for the man's sake. (10) Therefore the woman ought to have *a symbol of* authority on her head, because of the angels. (11) However, in the Lord, neither is woman independent of man, nor is man independent of woman. (12) For as the woman originates from the man, so also the man *has his birth* through the woman; and all things originate from God. (13) Judge for yourselves: is it proper for a woman to pray to God *with her head* uncovered? (14) Does not even nature itself teach you that if a man has long hair, it is a dishonor to him, (15) but if a woman has long hair, it is a glory to her? For her hair is given to her for a covering. (16) But if one is inclined to be contentious, we have no other practice, nor have the churches of God.

Notable Differences between Translations

To help you in your study, I'd like to point out the most significant translation differences between the New American Standard Bible (previous page) and other great English versions.

Verse 2: The King James Version translates the "traditions" as "ordinances."
Why does this matter? Some suggest that the "traditions" are the traditions of men. "Ordinances" more clearly communicates that they come from God. See chapter 2 for more information.

Verse 3: The English Standard Version translates "man/woman" as "husband/wife." They continue to use "wife" in every verse relating to women covering their heads in this chapter.
Why does this matter? Some believe that head covering is only for those who are married. By using marriage terms instead of generic words, the ESV supports that view in their translation. See chapter 13 for more information.

Verse 6: Instead of saying, if a woman does not cover her head she should have her hair "cut off," the ESV says "cut short."
Why does this matter? Verse 6 is a key passage that shows a problem with the view that a woman's long hair is the only covering that she needs. The ESV's rendering of "cut short" helps show the exegetical problem more clearly. See chapter 8 for more information.

Verse 16: The ESV, KJV, and NKJV say we have "no such practice" instead of "no other practice."
Why does this matter? Some suggest that this verse indicates that head covering was not the practice of the church.

Others point to this verse to show that all the churches practiced head covering. See chapter 6 for more information.

CHAPTER ONE

A History of Christian Head Covering

*"I do know this, that until fifty years ago, every
woman in every church covered her head. . . .
What has happened in the last fifty years? We've
had a feminist movement."*[4]
R.C. Sproul Jr., founder, Highlands Ministries;
Chair of Philosophy and Theology, Reformation
Bible College

Head covering is not a new doctrine. Since the time of the
apostles until the twentieth century, this practice was
upheld by most Christians. In fact, it still is the majority
view in much of the Eastern world. However, in the West
the practice has fallen out of favor and is now held only by
a minority. But this wasn't always the case.

Alice Morse Earle (American historian, 1851–1911)
documented in her book *Two Centuries of Costume in
America*, written more than one hundred years ago:
*"One singular thing may be noted in this history, –
that with all the vagaries of fashion, woman has never
violated the Biblical law that bade her cover her head.*

---

4. R.C. Sproul Jr. "Should Christians only sing Psalms in local
churches?" (Christianity.com video, 2012)
http://bit.ly/sproulpsalms.

9

She has never gone to church services bareheaded."[5]

So an American historian tells us that looking back on two hundred years of history, even though fashions changed, the one thing that did not was all Christian women covered their heads in church. Now, before we explore what happened for the practice to be largely abandoned, we need an overview of what the church has said about this symbol throughout the ages. Let's take a tour through history, starting with the early church, as we see what influential pastors and theologians have said about this practice.

The Early Church

Pre-Nicene Churches[6]

We learn from the writings of Tertullian (approx. AD 200) that the Corinthian church was still practicing head covering about 150 years after Paul wrote his letter to them. Tertullian said, *"So, too, did the Corinthians themselves understand [Paul]. In fact, at this day the Corinthians do veil their virgins. What the apostles taught, their disciples approve."*[7]

He also stated that it was practiced in other regions: *"Throughout Greece, and certain of its barbaric provinces, the majority of Churches keep their virgins covered. There are places, too, beneath this (African) sky, where this practice*

---

5. Alice Morse Earle, *Two Centuries of Costume in America,* vol. 2, 1620–1820. (New York: Macmillan, 1903), 582.

6.This refers to the time before the First Council of Nicaea in AD 325.

7. Tertullian. "On the Veiling of Virgins." ed. A. Roberts, J. Donaldson, and A. C. Coxe, trans.S. Thelwall, *Fathers of the Third Century: Tertullian,* Part Fourth; Minucius Felix; Commodian; Origen, Parts First and Second, vol. 4. (New York: Christian Literature Company, 1885), 33.

obtains." [8] Though his comments may give the impression that some churches did not practice head covering, it should be noted that he is speaking only of churches that veil all women, not only those who are married. Head covering for wives was not debated, but not everyone agreed with Tertullian that single women needed to be veiled too. So, as part of his case, he points to other areas where veiling virgins was the majority practice.

Irenaeus (AD 130–220), bishop of Lugdunum in Gaul (modern-day Lyon, France), was a disciple of Polycarp, who was a disciple of the apostle John. Irenaeus is the earliest church father to comment on head covering. He only does so in passing and, because of that, he does not articulate his view. However, he quotes 1 Corinthians 11:10 as *"A woman ought to have a veil upon her head, because of the angels."* [9] By saying "veil" instead of "authority" Irenaeus shows that he understood it to refer to a fabric covering, not a woman's long hair.

Clement of Alexandria (AD 150–215), a Christian theologian and dean of the Catechetical School of Alexandria, said, *"Woman and man are to go to church decently attired . . . for this is the wish of the Word, since it is becoming for her to pray veiled."* [10]

Hippolytus (AD 170–236), presbyter of the Church of Rome at the beginning of the third century, while giving instructions for church gatherings said, "Let all the women

---

8. Ibid.

9. Irenaeus of Lyons. "Irenæus against Heresies" in A. Roberts, J. Donaldson, and A. C. Coxe (Eds.), *The Apostolic Fathers with Justin Martyr and Irenaeus,* vol. 1. (New York: Christian Literature Company, 1885), 327.

10. Clement of Alexandria. "The Instructor" in *Fathers of the Second Century: Hermas, Tatian, Athenagoras, Theophilus, and Clement of Alexandria,* vol. 2, ed. A. Roberts, J. Donaldson, and A. C. Coxe (New York: Christian Literature Company, 1885), 290.

have their heads covered with an opaque cloth." [11]

Tertullian (approx. AD 155–225), a prolific writer and apologist from Carthage, North Africa, wrote the earliest and longest defense of head covering that we possess today. He said, *"I pray you, be you mother, or sister, or virgin-daughter—let me address you according to the names proper to your years—veil your head."*[12]

John Chrysostom (AD 347–407), the archbishop of Constantinople, wrote a commentary on 1 Corinthians 11. In this, he said, *"The business of whether to cover one's head was legislated by nature (see 1 Corinthians 11:14–15). When I say 'nature,' I mean 'God.' For he is the one who created nature. Take note, therefore, what great harm comes from overturning these boundaries! And don't tell me that this is a small sin."*[13]

Jerome (AD approx. 347–420), a renowned Christian scholar and theologian, is best known for translating the Bible into Latin (the Vulgate). He said that Christian women in Egypt and Syria do not *"go about with heads uncovered in defiance of the apostle's command, for they wear a close-fitting cap and a veil."*[14]

Augustine (AD 354–430), bishop of Hippo (modern-day Algeria), wrote theological books, including *The City of God* and *Confessions* which are still widely read today. He wrote, *"It is not becoming, even in married women, to uncover their hair, since the apostle commands women to keep their heads*

---

11. Hippolytus, and Easton, B. *The Apostolic Tradition of Hippolytus.* (New York: Macmillan, 1934), 43.

12. Tertullian, "On Veiling of Virgins," 37.

13. Judith L. Kovacs, *1 Corinthians: Interpreted by Early Christian Medieval Commentators* (*The Church's Bible*). (Michigan: Eerdmans, 2005), 180.

14. Jerome, "The Letters of St. Jerome," in *St. Jerome: Letters and Select Works*, vol. 6, ed. P. Schaff and H. Wace, trans. W. H. Fremantle, G. Lewis, and W. G. Martley (New York: Christian Literature Company, 1893), 292.

covered." [15]

The Middle Ages through the Twentieth Century

Church Councils

In various councils and synods throughout the early to middle ages, Paul's instructions in 1 Corinthians 11 were upheld as binding in the present day. A veil was ordered for women receiving the Eucharist during the fifth through the seventh centuries by the councils of Autun, Angers [16], and Auxerre.[17] The Synod of Rome in 743 said that *"[A] woman praying in church without her head covered brings shame upon her head, according to the word of the Apostle."* [18] Pope Nicholas I declared *ex cathedra* in 866 that *"The women must be veiled in church services."* [19]

Thomas Aquinas (1225–1274), an Italian Dominican friar, priest, and influential philosopher and theologian, is considered by the Catholic Church to be its greatest theologian and one of the thirty-three Doctors of the Church. He said, *"A veil put on the head designates the power of another over the head of a person existing in the order of nature. Therefore, the man existing under God should not*

---

15. Augustine of Hippo, "Letters of St. Augustin," in *The Confessions and Letters of St. Augustin with a Sketch of His Life and Work*, vol. 1, ed. P. Schaff, trans. J. G. Cunningham (New York: Christian Literature Company, 1886), 588.

16. John McClintock and James Strong, *Cyclopedia of Biblical, Theological and Ecclesiastical Literature*, vol. 10, (New York: Harper and Bros, 1891), 739.

17. Alvin J. Schmidt, *Veiled and Silenced*, (Macon, Georgia: Mercer University Press, 1989), 136. Schmidt's source is Carl Joseph Hefele, *Counciliengesshichte*, vol 3. (Freiburg: Herder'she Verlag, 1877), 46.

18. Synod of Rome, Canon 3, Giovanni Domenico Mansi, *Sacrorum Conciliorum Nova et Amplissima Collectio*, 382.

19. Alvin J. Schmidt, *Veiled and Silenced* (Macon, Georgia: Mercer University Press, 1989), 136.

have a covering over his to show he is immediately subject to God; but the woman should wear a covering to show that besides God she is naturally subject to another."[20]

William Tyndale (1494–1536), an English biblical scholar and foundational figure who translated the New Testament and the Pentateuch from the original languages into English, said, *"I answer, that Paul taught by mouth such things as he wrote in his epistles. And his traditions were . . . that a woman obey her husband, have her head covered, keep silence, and go womanly and Christianly appareled."*[21]

Martin Luther (1483–1546), a German theologian who was the catalyst behind the Protestant Reformation, said, *"The wife has not been created out of the head, so that she shall not rule over her husband, but be subject and obedient to him. For that reason the wife wears a headdress, that is, the veil on her head, as St. Paul writes in 1 Corinthians."*[22]

John Knox (1514–1572), a Scottish clergyman and leader in the Protestant Reformation, with five other reformers wrote the Scottish Confession of Faith and established the Reformed Presbyterian Church. He quoted John Chrysostom's writings advocating the practice of head covering and then shared his agreement by saying, *"True it is, Chrysostom."*[23]

---

20. Thomas Aquinas, *Super I Epistolam B. Pauli ad Corinthios lectura*, (608) Accessed at: http://dhspriory.org/thomas/SS1Cor.htm#111.

21. William Tyndale, *Doctrinal Treatises and Introductions to Different Portions of the Holy Scriptures*, ed. H. Walter, vol. 1, (Cambridge: Cambridge University Press, 1848), 219.

22. Martin Luther, "A Sermon on Marriage" (January 15, 1525) WA XVII/I.
in Susan C. Karant-Nunn and Merry E. Wiesner, *Luther on Women: A Sourcebook* (United Kingdom: Cambridge University Press, 2003), 95.

23. John Knox, "The First Blast of the Trumpet Against the Monstrous Regiment of Women" in *Selected Writings of John Knox: Public Epistles, Treatises, and Expositions to the Year 1559*

Charles Spurgeon (1834–1892), a Baptist pastor in London, is highly regarded cross-denominationally and is known as the "Prince of Preachers." He said, *"The reason why our sisters appear in the House of God with their heads covered is 'because of the angels.'"*[24]

Historical Summary

As we've seen, the attestation to the practice of head covering is documented from the second century and beyond. Many of Christianity's brightest and most influential theologians taught that the practice should be followed in their own culture and day. This is not a new doctrine—rather it is a teaching with a rich history that has only recently fallen out of practice.

Why Was It Abandoned?

In North America, head covering was practiced in virtually all churches up until the beginning of the twentieth century. This date is interesting because it coincides with the first wave of feminism. Although the practice continued in most churches, from that time forward it was a symbol in decline. Then in the 1960s and 70s, the number of women who practiced this symbol radically dropped. Once again, this coincided with another movement of feminism. During the 1960s, the Women's Liberation Movement swept America.

You may be wondering if the link between feminism and the decline of head covering is a mere coincidence. We know that it wasn't a coincidence because feminists were making organized efforts to try to eradicate the symbol. They understood that a woman covering her head was a symbol of her submission to male authority, and they hated

---

(Dallas, Texas, Presbyterian Heritage Publications), 1995.
24. Charles Spurgeon, *Spurgeon's Sermons on Angels,* (Michigan: Kregel Academic, 1996), 98.

that.

The National Organization for Women (NOW) is a feminist organization founded by Betty Friedan (author of *The Feminist Mystique*). In 1968 they rallied their troops to have a "national unveiling." Here's what they said:

"Because the wearing of a head covering by women at religious services is a symbol of subjection with many churches, NOW recommends that all chapters undertake an effort to have all women participate in a "national unveiling" by sending their head coverings to the task force chairman. At the spring meeting of the task force of women and religion, these veils will be publicly burned to protest the second class status of women in all churches." [25]

NOW rallied their various chapters to "undertake an effort" to stop the practice of head covering. They were so disgusted with the symbol and what it represented that they had a public burning of women's veils. Sadly, their efforts achieved what they hoped it would.

The New York Times also published an article showing how feminism was largely responsible for shutting down the industry of millinery (manufacturing of hats and headwear). They said: *"But as the beehive hairdo gained popularity in the 1960s and the feminist movement made it acceptable for women to leave their hats at home, the industry faded."* [26]

Theologian R.C. Sproul Sr. notes the disturbing connection as well: *"It does disturb me, that the . . . tradition of the woman covering her head in America did not pass away until we saw a cultural revolt against the authority of the*

---

25. National Organization for Women, Dec. 1968. Quotation taken from *The Power of the Positive Woman* by Phyllis Schlafly (New Rochelle, NY: Arlington House, 1977), 207

26. Carrie Budoff, "Headgear as a Footnote to History" *(New York Times,* April 6, 1997).

husband over the wife."[27]

We cannot be naive to the fact that we are influenced by the culture around us. Egalitarian thought has permeated the church, popularizing the beliefs that: Men and women serve no functional difference in the home. The man does not have a God-given responsibility to lead and the woman does not need to submit to her husband. Within the church, all offices are open to women.

This belief system, along with pressure from the culture, made the symbol of head covering fall out of favor until it was abandoned. Head covering was not innocently lost in North America, but is tied to the rejection of the biblical roles of men and women.

---

27. R.C. Sproul, "To Cover or Not To Cover" (from the series "The Hard Sayings of the Apostles"), http://bit.ly/sproulcover.

SECTION ONE

A BIBLICAL CASE FOR MODERN HEAD COVERING

CHAPTER TWO

Apostolic Tradition: Holding to What Has Been Delivered to Us

> *"When the apostles speak of tradition . . . they're not talking about human tradition, but they're talking about that which has been handed over from the apostles to the church. These were not traditions that were to be negotiated, this is God's tradition."* [28]
>
> Dr. R.C. Sproul Sr., founder, Ligonier Ministries

When we hear the word "tradition" we usually think of it as the inventions of man, which are not found in Scripture. The traditions may be beneficial (or at least not harmful), but because God doesn't command them, neither should we. When it comes to understanding head coverings we need to ask, is this a tradition or a command? Let's look at our first verse:

> *"Now I praise you because you remember me in everything and hold firmly to the traditions, just as I delivered them to you."* (1 Corinthians 11:2)

---

28. R.C. Sproul, "To Cover or Not To Cover" (from the series "The Hard Sayings of the Apostles"), http://bit.ly/sproulcover.

Though the "traditions" are not explicitly defined, we can safely conclude that head covering was one of them. Why do I believe this? The teaching on head covering (1 Corinthians 11:3–16) is sandwiched between two contrasting statements. In verse 2, Paul says "I praise you" followed by teaching on head coverings. Then in verse 17 he says "I do not praise you," followed by teaching on the Lord's Supper and spiritual gifts (which they were misusing). The sentence structure of 1 Corinthians 11 uses verses 2 and 17 as topic headings.

"I Praise You" (1 Cor 11:2)	"I Do Not Praise You" (1 Cor 11:17)
Head Covering (1 Cor 11:2–16)	The Lord's Supper (1 Cor 11:17–34) Spiritual Gifts (1 Cor 12:1–14:40)

What immediately follows each of those verses is a teaching on the practices that fit the heading; the first to inform (praise) and the latter to correct (praise not). If head covering was not being practiced by the Corinthians, it would have been addressed under the heading of "I do not praise you." So it wasn't that the Corinthians were not practicing head covering. We know they were because Paul said they "held firmly" to it. What they were lacking was "understanding," meaning they needed more teaching on this topic.

Now before you dismiss head covering as an invention of man, let's allow the Bible to give us our definition of tradition. The Greek word used is *paradosis*, which is used in the New Testament thirteen times. It is used eight times by Jesus, and every time He uses it clearly in reference to the "traditions of men." Paul also uses the term in this way, but not exclusively. Sometimes he uses it in reference to authoritative apostolic teaching. Let's look at two instances where he does that:

*"So then, brethren, stand firm and hold to the **traditions [paradosis]** which you were taught, whether by word of mouth or by letter from us."* (2 Thessalonians 2:15)

*"Now we command you, brethren, in the name of our Lord Jesus Christ, that you keep away from every brother who leads an unruly life and not according to the **tradition [paradosis]** which you received from us."* (2 Thessalonians 3:6)

Did you catch the pattern? When Paul uses *paradosis* to refer to apostolic teaching, he says it came "from us." So how do we know if head covering is the tradition of men or of the apostles? Paul doesn't leave us guessing. In 1 Corinthians 11:2 he says, *"I delivered [the traditions] to you."* This means that the practice of head covering is authoritative apostolic teaching.

To help visualize this, picture yourself opening your mailbox. You receive a dozen different letters, each delivered to you. One particular letter catches your attention because it's from the Internal Revenue Service. You give special attention to this letter because of whom the sender is. You understand that what they say in that letter has authority because it was given to them by the government. As you read it, you see that they are giving you instructions to fulfill. This cannot be ignored.

In the same way, this letter to the Corinthians is important because it was sent by an apostle with instructions for the church to uphold. This apostle is vested with authority by Jesus to lay the foundation of the church (Ephesians 2:20). More importantly, when he speaks in Scripture, God is speaking (2 Timothy 3:16).

Imagine yourself opening Paul's letter for the first time. You recognize its importance and start reading. He tells you in this letter that the reason he wrote you is so that you will have "understanding" regarding head covering. He wants you to know what the symbol means, why the churches practice it, and what it communicates when we ignore his instructions. You also see that he gives his praise if we "hold firmly" to teachings like this one. Let's continue looking through the apostle's letter together so we can see everything he wants us to "understand." In this next chapter we will look at the foundation of this symbol, which is the created order.

CHAPTER THREE

Creation Order: Manhood and Womanhood Symbolized

"The Christian doctrine of order in creation involving subordination requires the Christian practice of manifesting that order in public worship by the veiling of women." [29]
Dr. Charles Ryrie, editor, *The Ryrie Study Bible*; former professor at Dallas Theology Seminary

When a new believer is baptized, this symbolizes death to the old life and the person's new life in Christ (Romans 6:4). This practice of baptism is significant primarily because of the meaning invested in it. Likewise, head covering also symbolizes something great. Let's take a look at the foundation of this practice to find out what is communicated when men worship with uncovered heads and women with theirs veiled.

> *"But I want you to understand that Christ is the head of every man, and the man is the head of a woman, and God is the head of Christ."* (1 Corinthians 11:3)

---

29. Charles Ryrie, *The Role of Women in the Church*, 2nd ed., chap. 8, (Nashville: B&H Publishing, 2011).

God has made men and women equal in value and worth. They both need each other, or, as the Scriptures say, *"in the Lord, neither is woman independent of man, nor is man independent of woman"* (1 Corinthians 11:11).

But just because male and female are equal does not mean that they have the same role, authority, or function.[30] These differences can be seen throughout Creation, in angels, and even in God Himself. The doctrine of the Trinity is that there is only one God, revealed in three distinct persons: the Father, the Son, and the Holy Spirit. These three persons are all fully God and fully equal, but they are distinct in function, authority, and person. As we have seen in the above verse, *"God is the head of Christ."* This submission of Jesus to the Father was not limited to His incarnation. Rather, the Scriptures say:

> *"When all things are subjected to Him, then the Son Himself also will be subjected to the One who subjected all things to Him, so that God may be all in all."* (1 Corinthians 15:28)

So even though right now the Father has *"put all things in subjection under [Christ's] feet"* (1 Corinthians 15:27), after Jesus returns He will still be subject to the Father. Don't miss this: the Son will submit to the Father for all eternity.

Jesus is not less valuable than the Father. The Holy Spirit is not less valuable than Jesus, even though His role is not to speak about Himself but instead to glorify the Son (John 16:13).

Different roles do not have to mean different value or

---

30. I am defending a view called complementarianism. The opposing view is called egalitarianism. To read more on this topic, see *Men and Women: Equal Yet Different: A Brief Study of the Biblical Passages on Gender* by Alexander Strauch (Colorado Springs: Lewis and Roth Publishers, 1999).

worth. This point can't be stressed highly enough. Does a police officer have an authority over you given by God (Romans 13:1)? Yes! Is that police officer of more value or worth than you as a human? No! Children submit to their parents (Ephesians 6:1); slaves submit to their masters (Ephesians 6:5); wives submit to their husbands (Ephesians 5:22); citizens submit to their government (Romans 13:1); church members submit to their elders (Hebrews 13:17); and Jesus submits to God (1 Corinthians 11:3). There are even different ranks in the angels, as Michael is called the archangel (Jude 9), meaning "chief."

We need not be afraid of authority. There will be lousy parents, brutal masters, chauvinist husbands, power-tripping pastors, and ungodly governments until the end. That's because of sin, though, not because authority is bad. Let us look to the Trinity as our model and example.

So the foundational reason for head covering is the created order. This means that woman submits to man, man submits to Christ, and Christ submits to the Father. This is the authority structure that God has ordered, and because of that, it is good. This is the message that Paul said "I want you to understand" (1 Corinthians 11:3).

Before we examine the next verse about the created order I want to challenge my complementarian [31] friends. I know the arguments you use for male eldership and husband headship. I agree with you fully. In 1 Timothy 2 it explains why a woman cannot *"teach or exercise authority,"* doesn't it?

"But I do not allow a woman to teach or exercise authority over a man, but to remain quiet. For it was Adam who was first created, and then Eve. And it was not Adam who was deceived, but the woman being

---

31 The view that men and women complement each other through their differences in role, authority, and function. This is the position I hold.

deceived, fell into transgression." (1 Timothy 2:12–14)

"The reason is based in Creation," you would say, "therefore it isn't cultural." Agreed. But now I want to challenge you to remain consistent as we examine this next verse.

"For a man ought not to have his head covered, since he is the image and glory of God; but the woman is the glory of man. For man does not originate from woman, but woman from man; for indeed man was not created for the woman's sake, but woman for the man's sake. Therefore the woman ought to have a symbol of authority on her head." (1 Corinthians 11:7–10a)

Paul says why women must have a symbol of authority on their head—because of the created order.

Where do you find man being directly created in the image of God? It's found in Genesis 1.

Where do you find woman being created from man, or being the "glory of man"? That's in Genesis 2.

Where do you find that the woman was created for man, not the other way around? Once again, that's in Genesis 2.

And when do you find sin entering the picture? Not until Genesis 3.

So this foundation is not only based in Creation, it is based in God's perfect Creation before sin. Headship and authority is God's original intent. It isn't a post-Fall disaster, but a pre-Fall masterpiece.

Some argue that submission and authority is a curse from the Fall, based on Genesis 3:16, which says, *"Your desire will be for your husband, and he will rule over you."* This verse isn't introducing post-Fall roles but rather explaining how the Fall is going to negatively affect our roles. Women would now struggle with a desire for their husband's position of authority, and husbands would be tempted to tyrannically rule over their wives. The curse is a distortion of God's order, one we must war against.

There are numerous indications of Adam's headship found in the first two chapters of Genesis. Remember, this is before sin entered the world. When God said that He was going to create woman, He referred to her as a *"helper suitable for [man]"* (Genesis 2:18). This shows her created function. She was to help, not rule.

Likewise, it was Adam who named Eve "woman" (Genesis 2:23). We understand that the one who does the naming has an authority over the one named. We show this when we name our children, and Adam showed this when he named the animals and Eve. Finally, we see that even though Adam and Eve both sinned, and both received a punishment, it was Adam who bore the responsibility. The Scriptures state that *"in Adam all die"* (1 Corinthians 15:22) and that *"through one man sin entered into the world"* (Romans 5:12). Sin is never said to have come from Eve because she did not have headship. The leader is the one who bears the responsibility, even if someone under him does something wrong.

Here is a summary of the created differences between men and women. This is why one gender must wear a symbol of authority (head covering) and the other must not.

Men (Uncovered)	Women (Covered)
Man is the head of woman. (1 Cor 11:3)	Women submit to the proper male authority in their lives as head. (1 Cor 11:3)
Man was created directly by God from the dust and is the "glory of God." (1 Cor 11:7–8)	Woman was created by God from man's rib and is the "glory of man." (1 Cor 11:7–8)
Man was not created for the woman's sake. (1 Cor 11:9)	Woman was created for the man's sake. (1 Cor 11:9)

God in his infinite wisdom has selected perfect symbols to display this difference in the created order. Our God loves communicating through symbols: He gave us the spotless lamb, the unleavened bread, the water in baptism, the bread and wine, the olive tree, marriage, the temple, the feasts, and the list could go on and on. One can't help but think of Ezekiel having to lie on his side for 390 days (Ezekiel 4), Isaiah walking naked and barefoot for three years (Isaiah 20:3), or Hosea having to marry a prostitute (Hosea 1:2). God could have just declared His message through those prophets, but He desired to use them as living symbols too.

Each symbol in Scripture was chosen by God for a specific purpose to point to a greater reality. In the Book of Hebrews we see this with regards to the tent that Moses was commanded to make.

> "For when Moses was about to erect the tent, he was instructed by God, saying, 'See that you make everything according to the pattern that was shown you on the mountain.'" (Hebrews 8:5 ESV)

The author later points out that the tent is a symbol "of this present age" (Hebrews 9:9 ESV). Even though it was a symbol, Moses was still given very specific instructions and was told to follow them. The reason being, if the symbol is changed it no longer accurately reflects what God was using it to point to. So it is with head covering.

Dr. Bruce Waltke rightly warns:

> "A woman who prays or prophesies in an assembly of believers should cover her head as a symbol of her submission to the absolute will of God who has ordered His universe according to His own good pleasure. The picture of His rule must not be seized by believers into their own hands to shape it according to their own pleasure."[32]

---

32. Bruce K. Waltke, "1 Corinthians 11:2–16: An Interpretation" (*Bibliotheca Sacra* 135:537, Jan. 1978), 56.

So the man reflects the glory of God and his submission to Christ by praying and prophesying with a bare head. The woman reflects the glory of man and her submission to the proper male authority in her life by praying and prophesying with her head covered. If we change the symbol or abandon it altogether, we miss out on displaying to men and angels the wisdom of God in Creation.

In the next chapter we will try to determine what Paul meant when he said that women cover their heads *"because of the angels,"* and I'll also show what this argument means for the cultural view.

CHAPTER FOUR

Angels: Considering the Heavenly Host

"The Scripture teaches that when Christians meet together, and when they gather together in prayer, then the angels of God are present, and the women are to be covered when they take part in public prayer because of the presence of the angels. It is a tremendous and a remarkable thing."[33]
Dr. Martyn Lloyd-Jones, former minister of Westminster Chapel, London

When it comes to verses that Christians admit they don't understand, 1 Corinthians 11:10 tops most of our lists. Here's what that passage says:

"Therefore the woman ought to have a symbol of authority on her head, because of the angels."

The apostle Paul just told us that women are to cover their heads because of the angels. So no matter what this verse means in its fullness, what we know is we have one of his reasons for practicing this symbol. This point can't be stressed highly enough. We don't seek to understand what

---

33. Martyn Lloyd Jones, *Great Doctrines of the Bible*, (Carol Stream, Illinois: Crossway Books, 2003), 110.

this verse means so that if we do "get it" it will become evidence for head covering. Rather, because it is a reason, we therefore seek to understand it.

The difficulty for us is that Paul says this in passing without explaining what he meant. A likely reason for this is that the church in Corinth understood what Paul meant, therefore an explanation would be unnecessary. In his letter to the Thessalonians, he said that he had explained details about Christ's Second Coming to them when he was with them (2 Thessalonians 2:5). This too may be one of those doctrines articulated while in their presence.

Since this is a very short and vague verse, there's no way we can know with absolute certainty what it means. However, we're not left totally in the dark. There is an indication in the Greek that helps us identify which angels Paul meant. There are also other Scriptures about these beings that I believe shed light on this passage. Let's start by identifying if Paul was speaking about good or evil angels.

Angels: Good or Evil?

In grammar, the definite article is used to modify a noun. It takes a person, place, or thing and indicates that you are not referring to the noun generally, but have a specific reference in mind. This definite article shows up in English as the word "the." So, as an example, if I were to say "she loves chocolate," it is a very broad use and could refer to all chocolate. However, by adding the definite article it transforms the sentence to "she loves *the* chocolate." This indicates to the reader that the chocolate being referred to is a specific kind.

The Greek language also has the definite article [34] and in 1 Corinthians 11:10 it is used where Paul says *"because of*

---

34. In English there are both definite and indefinite articles. In Greek such a distinction doesn't exist so it's actually just an "article."

the *angels.*" This indicates that Paul is not talking about *all* angels but has has *specific* ones in mind. According to Dr. David E. Garland, *"Paul never uses the word 'angels' with the definite article to refer to bad angels."* [35] Likewise, Robertson and Plummer affirm *"evil angels [cannot] be meant; the article is against it:* ἄγγελος *always mean good angels."* [36] So whatever Paul meant by women having a symbol of authority on their heads "because of the angels," it is likely that he had the holy angels in mind.

Now that we've identified what type of angels, we need to figure out why Paul said that we practice this symbol because of them. Through examining relevant verses on angels we're going to end up with two possible conclusions to explain this verse. Both conclusions could be right since they don't contradict each other, but it may be that Paul meant only one.

For Their Benefit

The purpose of head covering is to provide a visual symbol of God's created order to the gathered church. If angels are a reason why we obey this command, it presupposes that they must be watching us worship. One understanding of why we practice head covering is so that we may rightly symbolize the created order to all present, both visible and invisible. Paul says:

"So that through the church the manifold wisdom of

---

35. David E. Garland, *First Corinthians* (Baker Academic, 2003), 527.

36. Archibald T. Robertson and Alfred Plummer, *A Critical and Exegetical Commentary on the First Epistle of St. Paul to the Corinthians* (T&T Clark, 1911), 233.
(When they mention "ἄγγελος always means good angels," this must be understood as when the word is used with the Greek article in Paul's letters.)

God might now be made known to the rulers and the authorities in the heavenly places." (Ephesians 3:10 ESV)

These rulers and authorities are the angels of God (Colossians 1:16; 1 Peter 3:22). We see from this passage that what our Lord is doing through the church shows to them how incredibly wise He is. Peter describes the angels as *"longing to look"* into what God is doing (1 Peter 1:12). They are captivated by what God is doing and want to see more of it. I believe this is a desire God would take pleasure in fulfilling. Allowing angels to watch us worship could be one way of fulfilling that desire.

I love thinking about what the angels must be thinking, since they have such a unique perspective. The angels were the very first of God's creation. We know they have seen all of history unfold because God told Job that the angels rejoiced watching Him make the world (Job 38:4–7).

The angels have spent their entire lives in the presence of a holy and perfect God. They watched Him create a perfect world, where there was no sin, death, or suffering. Those concepts were unknown to them. Then one of their own, Satan, rebelled against God. God put him and the angels who followed him out of His presence forever (Jude 6). No opportunities for repentance and no one to intercede on their behalf. The angels know that sin has a high cost.

Then, as a repeat, the first couple God created also sins. However, there's a twist in this storyline. God kills an animal in their place and promises them a Redeemer. He then sets apart a group of these sinful humans to display His love and affection. It culminates in God Himself entering the world in human flesh. The Savior lives a perfect life and then lays it down as an unblemished sacrifice. The Father slaughters Him, the Lamb of God, so that ill-deserving children of the devil can be totally forgiven and adopted into His family. What a story! No wonder the angels long to look into this.

Now, put yourself in their shoes as they watch the gathered people of God worship.

They see enemies of God now worshiping because they have been forgiven and redeemed. They see Jews and Gentiles worshiping together as members of one body in unity. They see males and females worshiping together as equals. In addition to all that, through head covering, our women show all present that their position as a woman is also redeemed. No longer are they at war, usurping and longing for the man's position of authority (Genesis 3:16). Instead they are content in the role God ordained for them in Genesis 2.

The men, likewise, by their bare heads, communicate that they will exercise authority in their respective role. However, no longer will it be through domineering (Genesis 3:16) or being passive like the first Adam. Their position as a man is also redeemed.

As they watch this, the angels must cry out, "Behold the manifold wisdom of God!"

Let's not forget that as sinless beings they would be much more sensitive to sin. If we are dishonorable and disgraceful from a human perspective (1 Corinthians 11:4–6), how must we look to angels if we disobey this command? If we don't pray and prophesy as God said to, the only thing we may be symbolizing to them is the role distortion of Genesis 3!

For Our Benefit

The Scriptures also seem to imply that angels may be reporting to God whether or not we're obeying Him. Let me explain what I mean. On judgment day we have to give an account for everything that we have said (Matthew 12:36) or done (1 Corinthians 3:13). So God must be keeping a record. Also, there are verses that speak of ways our prayers are hindered, such as neglecting the poor (Proverbs 21:13) and being a bad husband (1 Peter 3:7). Those are sins that must be observed, recorded, and reported.

Now, God is omniscient so He knows all things. However, He can choose to use specific means to receive this information if He desires. For example, God chooses to judge the dead *"by what was written in the books, according to what they had done"* (Revelation 20:12 ESV). He doesn't need a book, but He chooses to use one to record the deeds of people. In the same way, God doesn't need anyone or anything to let Him know who is being obedient to His commands, but there is scriptural implication that the Father chooses to have this information presented to Him by angels. Here's what Jesus said:

> *"See that you do not despise one of these little ones, for I say to you that their angels in heaven continually see the face of My Father who is in heaven."* (Matthew 18:10)

When a child is sinned against, God doesn't just say, "I know about it." He says their angel comes before Him. The implication is that the angel would be reporting to God what had happened.

Let's look at another verse:

> *"In the presence of God and of Christ Jesus and of the elect angels I charge you to keep these rules without prejudging, doing nothing from partiality."* (1 Timothy 5:21 ESV)

As Paul left Timothy with commands, he reminded him that what was ordered was done *"in the presence of the elect angels."* It's as if he was saying "the angels are witnesses of what I've commanded you, and they will be watching." Understanding that we are being observed and held accountable serves to sober us in our efforts in obedience. Our lives are not private, but are lived out before a cosmic audience.

Now, even if I've missed it on my explanation, the reason is still clear: we're to obey *"because of the angels."* Children can hypothesize why their dad asked them to do such-and-such a command, but the main point shouldn't be missed. Regardless of the reason, both the command and the person who wants obedience are very clear.

Getting the Audience Right

I want to end with one last point. Later (in chapter 9) we will discuss the popular view that the practice of head covering was only for that culture. That argument is built on the premise that this symbol is only for humans and it was important so as to not offend their local customs. But here Paul directly contradicts that sentiment by showing us that we do it for a completely different group of beings. This practice is not just a witness to people, but for angels, who do not change and do not have cultural practices. This, then, is a strong reason for why head covering is timeless and transcultural.

As we proceed through Paul's letter, let's turn our attention to what he says about nature and how this bears witness through our hair lengths that the practice of head covering is right.

CHAPTER FIVE

Nature: What Our Hair Teaches Us about Head Covering

"Long hair is an indication from 'nature' of the differentiation between men and women, and so the head covering required is in line with what 'nature' teaches."[37]
John Murray, professor, Westminster Theological Seminary, 1930–66

Paul's argument about *nature* is probably the most confusing and misunderstood of all his reasons. He appeals to a person's sense of what is right, based upon what nature teaches us about our hair lengths. Here's what he says:

"Judge for yourselves: is it proper for a woman to pray to God with her head uncovered? Does not even nature itself teach you that if a man has long hair, it is a dishonor to him, but if a woman has long hair, it is a glory to her? For her hair is given to her for a

---

37. John Murray, "Head Coverings and Decorum in Worship: A Letter to Mr. V. Connors" accessed April 27, 2015, on http://www.headcoveringmovement.com/articles/head-coverings-and-decorum-in-worship-a-letter-by-john-murray.

covering." (1 Corinthians 11:13–15)

A rhetorical question, according to *The Merriam-Webster Dictionary*, is *"asked in order to make a statement rather than to get an answer."* This is what Paul is doing when he asks, "Is it proper?" We know this primarily because he just finished a lengthy defense for why we must practice head covering. He would not then overturn that by allowing others to choose if they want to obey a doctrine rooted in Creation. Rather, Paul is declaring the debate closed. He is saying, "You all know this is the only right option." No one would say that it's proper for a woman to pray uncovered in church. The reason they would all agree is because they understood that a head covering in this context is a sign of biblical femininity. It visibly proclaims that a woman joyfully accepts God's authority structure for her life.

Some people think that when Paul says "judge for yourselves" he's saying that we have the freedom to decide if women should pray covered or not. To show that this is not what he meant, let's examine a few similar passages.

"I speak as to sensible people; **judge for yourselves** *what I say. The cup of blessing that we bless, is it not a participation in the blood of Christ? The bread that we break, is it not a participation in the body of Christ?"* (1 Corinthians 10:15–16 ESV)

When Paul asks the Corinthians to *"judge for yourselves,"* is he saying that there are two perfectly fine options and they just need to pick the one that works best for them? That one in taking Communion participates in both the blood and body of Christ, but the other not? Or, rather, is the answer implied that Communion is participation in Christ?

"But Peter and John answered and said to them,

*'Whether it is right in the sight of God to give heed to you rather than to God, **you be the judge**; for we cannot stop speaking about what we have seen and heard.'"* (Acts 4:19–20)

When Peter and John ask the council to *"be the judge,"* are they saying that there are two perfectly fine options? One chooses to obey God, but the other chooses to heed man's instruction? Or, rather, is the answer implied that, yes, we must obey God rather than man? You be the judge.

So, just like the other examples, Paul is not giving two equal options. He just finished saying *"every woman who has her head uncovered while praying or prophesying disgraces her head"* (1 Corinthians 11:5). The answer to Paul's question is implied: it is not proper for a woman to pray uncovered, which is why he said, *"Let her cover her head"* (1 Corinthians 11:6).

Defining Nature

Now Paul moves on from his rhetorical question to an argument about what "nature" teaches us. In order to understand his argument correctly, we first need to define what the word nature (Greek: *physis*) means. The BDAG [38] lexicon says it is the *"the regular or established order of things,"* [39] and the Abbott-Smith lexicon says it's *"the regular order or law of nature."* [40] So we're talking about things that are intrinsic. Next, I want to take you a little deeper and actually look at how Paul uses this word in another passage.

---

38. BDAG stands for Bauer, Danker, Arndt, and Gingrich. This is their Greek-English Lexicon of the New Testament.

39. W. Arndt, F. W. Danker, and W. Bauer, *A Greek-English Lexicon of the New Testament and Other Early Christian literature*, 3rd ed. (Chicago: University of Chicago Press, 2000), 1070.

40. G. Abbott-Smith, *A Manual Greek Lexicon of the New Testament* (New York: Charles Scribner's Sons, 1922), 476.

He says:

> *"For when Gentiles, who do not have the law, by* **nature [physis]** *do what the law requires, they are a law to themselves, even though they do not have the law. They show that the work of the law is written on their hearts, while their conscience also bears witness, and their conflicting thoughts accuse or even excuse them."* (Romans 2:14–15 ESV)

Here Paul teaches that humans by "nature" have an inborn sense of right and wrong. He further says that "nature" lines up with God's written Law. Since that is the case, it would be erroneous to define it as a cultural opinion because that often is contrary to what God has declared. In the New Testament, *physis* appears fourteen times, and, each time it's used, it always refers to a part of God's Creation or the established order. This means men having short hair, and women wearing theirs longer, is not a cultural invention but is a part of the natural order, which is meant to distinguish between the sexes.

What Our Hair Teaches

Now that we understand that "nature" is God's established order, we need to figure out why Paul starts speaking about hair lengths and how he sees that as supporting his argument [41] for head covering. Let's take a look at our verse again:

> *"Judge for yourselves: is it proper for a woman to pray to God with her head uncovered? Does not even nature*

---

41. Some believe that Paul is not supporting his argument, but rather defining it. This means they disagree that Paul was ever speaking about an artificial covering and only had hair lengths in mind. I cover this objection in chapter eight.

> *itself teach you that if a man has long hair, it is a dishonor to him, but if a woman has long hair, it is a glory to her? For her hair is given to her for a covering."* (1 Corinthians 11:13–15)

Paul says that we know it is right for women to pray covered since nature has already shown that it's fitting by giving women a natural covering of hair. So the command for an artificial covering (at specific times) is in line with what she already possesses (all the time.) In the same way, it is right for men to pray uncovered because natural propriety has determined that men must keep their hair short, so that it does not become a covering.

This command to pray uncovered (at specific times) is in line with what nature has determined for them (all the time). Furthermore, hair lengths are meant to distinguish between the sexes, and Paul says that when we disregard this by men having long hair and women having short hair,[42] that dishonors a person. This, too, is in line with his teaching for how we are to worship, since women who pray uncovered and men who pray covered both dishonor their heads (1 Corinthians 11:4–5).

---

42. "Long" must be understood as in contrast to the length of men's short hairstyles wherever one lives. Just like dressing modestly, there are some outfits that clearly do not fit the label no matter the culture. Likewise, there are some hairstyles that could not be called "long" no matter where one lives. However, there is a fair amount of subjectivity to it as well. When a woman's hair is called a covering (1 Corinthian 11:15), the Greek word used is *peribolaion*. This word indicates something that can be "wrapped around." So men should keep their hair short enough that it cannot be wrapped around their heads.

Gender	How one is to appear when "praying and prophesying" (1 Cor 11:4–5)	How one is to appear in everyday life (1 Cor 11:14–15)	What happens if someone disregards these gender distinctions (1 Cor 11:4–5, 14–15)
Men	Uncovered (nothing artificial on their head)	Uncovered (by their hair kept short)	Dishonor
Women	Covered (something artificial that covers their head)	Covered (by their hair kept long)	Dishonor

Homosexuality and Hair

Now I know you're probably thinking, *Could there be anything less significant in the sight of God than how we wear our hair?* It's true that, comparatively speaking, this is minor. But I want to encourage you not to treat something as insignificant if the Word of God says that it is dishonorable if you disobey (1 Corinthians 11:4–5).

We also need to treat the matter seriously if we're going to be consistent in upholding heterosexuality as natural. This example is important to this discussion because the apostle Paul condemned both homosexuality and men wearing their hair long using the same Greek words. He says both are against nature (*physis*) and both are dishonorable/disgraceful (*atimia*). Look at these two passages side by side, paying close attention to the Greek words in brackets.

> *"For this reason God gave them up to **dishonorable** [**atimia**] passions. For their women exchanged natural relations for those that are contrary to **nature** [**physis**]; and the men likewise gave up natural*

relations with women and were consumed with passion for one another." (Romans 1:26–27 ESV)

*"Does not **nature [physis]** itself teach you that if a man wears long hair it is a **disgrace [atimia]** for him, but if a woman has long hair, it is her glory? For her hair is given to her for a covering."* (1 Corinthians 11:14–15 ESV)

In these two passages we have the same author (Paul), making the same moral judgment (dishonorable), by appealing to the same reason (nature). So if we are to be consistent, we must treat both the same. Now, to clarify, this is not to say that both are equally dishonorable. Paul also taught us that there are different degrees of sin, with sexual sin being on its own level (1 Corinthians 6:18). However, what we can't say is that one of these passages refers to a cultural invention while the other is established by God. In the Western world today, homosexuality has become culturally acceptable, as has short hair on women and long hair on men. However, just because culture allows a practice, that does not make it right.

Summary

So while head covering is taught explicitly in Scripture, it is confirmed by what nature silently teaches as well. It shows us that the hair given to each sex confirms the appropriateness of head covering since the two are in line with each other. It also teaches us that it is dishonorable when we disregard a gender distinction. Just as it is inappropriate to do that with our hair lengths, so it is with head covering while "praying and prophesying."

Now as we continue to move through Paul's letter, we will find that head covering was not limited to the Corinthian congregation, but was the practice of *every* church.

CHAPTER SIX

Church Practice: The Exclusive View of the Early Churches

"Paul taught all the churches this custom and he expected them to follow it. In this final statement he cuts off all further argument by appealing to universal Christian usage."[43]
Mary A. Kassian, Professor of Women's Studies, Southern Baptist Theological Seminary

Paul's final word regarding head covering provides one of the strongest arguments in favor of it: the uniform practice of all churches. Here is what he says:

"If anyone is inclined to be contentious, we have no such practice, nor do the churches of God." (1 Corinthians 11:16" ESV)

While most people in the Corinthian church held to the practice of head covering, there were obviously a few who had problems with it. Paul tells these people that, if they are going to be contentious, they stand alone. All the apostles

---

43. Mary Kassian, *Women, Creation and the Fall* (Crossway Books, 1990), 100.

and every local church held to the practice of head covering.

No Such Practice?

You may wonder, why I say they held to the practice of head covering when what he actually says is they have *"no such practice"*? In order to solve this apparent discrepancy, we must define "practice" by looking to its closest antecedent. We understand that if I said, *"He doesn't want to go there,"* you can only know who "he" is and where "there" is by looking to the previous sentence(s) to find the antecedents of those words. Likewise, we can only know what the "practice" is by looking to the previous verses. That is the key to rightly interpreting this passage. Let's start at verse 13 so you can see this for yourself.

> *"Judge for yourselves: is it proper for a wife to pray to God with her head uncovered? Does not nature itself teach you that if a man wears long hair it is a disgrace for him, but if a woman has long hair, it is her glory? For her hair is given to her for a covering. If anyone is inclined to be contentious, we have no such practice, nor do the churches of God."* (1 Corinthians 11:13–16 ESV)

The start of this verse where he says "judge for yourselves" is the start of a new thought. He is giving a new argument from nature, and he does this by asking the rhetorical question, *"Is it proper for a woman to pray uncovered?"* This is the question under discussion. He then proceeds to make his argument by pointing to hair lengths before we arrive at the verse we've been talking about. So it should be noted that the closest antecedent for "practice" is not head covering, which hasn't been mentioned since verse 10, but rather it is practice of women praying uncovered (1 Corinthians 11:13).

So Paul is saying that if someone is being contentious, the churches have "no such practice" as that which the contentious person is advocating for (that is, women praying uncovered). Paul is not saying that there is no official position on head covering—he just finished giving that defense. That's why other versions try to make this verse more readable by translating it, *"We have no other practice, nor have the churches of God"* (1 Corinthians 11:16). It's less literal, but it tries to bring out the true meaning more clearly. [44]

Beyond Corinth

Some argue that Paul commanded women to wear a head covering because of a local situation in Corinth. However, in this verse (1 Corinthians 11:16) Paul shows that this goes beyond Corinth and is the practice of all churches everywhere. Just think of the churches that were in existence at this time: Corinth, Philippi, Thessalonica, Ephesus, Iconium, Caesarea, Antioch, and many more. They all practiced head covering. All these churches would have a mixture of Jews and Gentiles fellowshipping in them and have people from different cultures. They are spread out geographically over thousands of miles in such places as modern-day Israel, Turkey, and Greece. Yet, they all held to the same Christian doctrine regarding head covering. How can such unity be accounted for except the church understanding head covering as a command for all Christians?

The Church in Corinth 150 Years Later

---

44. The NASB footnotes state that "no such practice" is the literal reading. They give a less literal translation for the sake of readability. So in their translation it assumes the practice is head covering.

Tertullian, a Christian apologist who lived from around AD 155 to 220, wrote many theological books. In one, *The Veiling of Virgins*, he argued from Scripture and tradition that all women are to be covered, not only those who are married. There is one very helpful statement that he made about the church in Corinth in his day, approximately 150 years after Paul wrote his first letter to them. He says:

> *"So, too, did the Corinthians themselves understand [Paul]. In fact, at this day the Corinthians do veil their virgins. What the apostles taught, their disciples approve."* [45]

Having observed the third century Corinthian church, Tertullian in essence says, *"They understood that Paul meant all women must wear head coverings. That's evidenced by the fact that to this day this is still their practice."*

This teaching remained the standard practice of most churches throughout the majority of church history. As R.C. Sproul Sr. notes, *"The wearing of fabric head coverings in worship was universally the practice of Christian women until the twentieth century. What happened? Did we suddenly find some biblical truth to which the saints for thousands of years were blind? Or were our biblical views of women gradually eroded by the modern feminist movement that has infiltrated the Church of Jesus Christ, which is 'the pillar and ground of the truth'?"* [46]

Head covering is not some new, strange doctrine. This is an old doctrine, based in the Bible and understood that way by the majority throughout the history of the church. Head covering was practiced in all churches through the centuries, and we are the exception today. It's time to

---

45. Tertullian, "On the Veiling of Virgins," 33.

46. Greg Price, "Head coverings in Scripture," http://www.albatrus.org/english/living/modesty/headcoverings_in_scripture.htm, accessed Aug. 23, 2015.

change that.

We have one final consideration before we end the biblical case for head covering. I'm going to show you five reasons why this practice is a biblical command, not a matter of Christian liberty.

CHAPTER SEVEN

Prescriptive: Why This Practice Isn't Christian Liberty

"Because of the woman's place dictated by creation, she ought to have power on her head (v. 10). The word translated 'ought' both here and in verse 7 is a strong term expressing obligation or duty; consequently, there is no option or choice in the matter."[47]
Dr. Michael Barrett, professor, Puritan Reformed Theological Seminary

Christian liberty is a Christian's right to make a decision on issues that are not commanded by God. With these types of issues there are biblical parameters that limit our choices and biblical principles that should inform our choices, but there is not only one correct answer for all Christians. This idea is taught in Romans 14 where the apostle Paul says:

"One person believes he may eat anything, while the

---

47. Michael P.V. Barrett, "Head Covering for Public Worship: An Exposition of 1 Corinthians 11:2–16," http://www.headcoveringmovement.com/Michael-Barrett-Head-Covering-for-Public-Worship.pdf (Faith Free Presbyterian Church, 2003), accessed May 3, 2016.

weak person eats only vegetables. Let not the one who eats despise the one who abstains, and let not the one who abstains pass judgment on the one who eats, for God has welcomed him. Who are you to pass judgment on the servant of another? It is before his own master that he stands or falls. And he will be upheld, for the Lord is able to make him stand. One person esteems one day as better than another, while another esteems all days alike. Each one should be fully convinced in his own mind. The one who observes the day, observes it in honor of the Lord. The one who eats, eats in honor of the Lord, since he gives thanks to God, while the one who abstains, abstains in honor of the Lord and gives thanks to God." (Romans 14:2–6 ESV)

Paul says that God doesn't command a certain diet or ask us to esteem certain days. Therefore, one person can eat vegetarian while another can eat meat. One can observe a day as special while another can treat all days alike. Both can hold to their contrary views while bringing glory of God. Some other areas that would be considered a Christian's liberty would be their style of fashion, what media they take in (television, music, news), and how they vote in elections. These issues will have scriptural parameters and principles to help guide our choices, but there is no command that would only allow for one view.

So, in summary, an area of Christian liberty 1) is not commanded by God and 2) allows for Christians to hold contrary positions while still glorifying God.

Is Head Covering Christian Liberty?

In 1 Corinthians 11, head covering is defended as a biblical imperative to bring conformity in practice (verse 16). Because of this I don't believe it would be right to classify it as a matter of Christian liberty. Here are five reasons why I understand head covering as a command:

1. Head covering is a teaching that was "held firmly" by the church because it was delivered with apostolic authority (1 Corinthians 11:2). Liberty issues are left to the Christian, not delivered to the churches for them to hold to.
2. Paul tells anyone who would disagree with head covering that the churches have only one view, and that's their practice of it (1 Corinthians 11:16). Liberty issues are marked by multiple views, not an exclusive position.
3. The sentence structure commands an action: *"But since it is disgraceful for a wife to cut off her hair or shave her head, let her cover her head"* (1 Corinthians 11:6 ESV). Liberty issues are marked by the absence of a direct action-command.
4. Paul says that to not practice head covering is dishonorable, disgraceful, and comparable to a woman having a shaved head (1 Corinthians 11:4–6). Liberty issues are marked by a plurality of choices that can bring glory to God, while Paul says in this instance only one choice can.
5. Paul defends head covering by appealing to the creation order, nature, and the angels. Liberty issues are marked by their silence in the Scriptures, not by a defense.

For these reasons I believe head covering is a biblical command that should be practiced by all Christians.

We "Ought" to Practice It

Some have suggested that head covering is not a biblical command because Paul tells us that we "ought" to practice it, not that we must. The Greek word behind "ought" is *opheilō*, and it occurs thirty-five times in the New Testament. In its various occurrences it is translated as owed, obligated, ought, should, and even must (with a few other words that are closely related). In all instances, *opheilō* is meant to lead the person to one practice only. It does not carry the connotation of choice, but of obligation.

For example, Paul says, *"Husbands ought also to love their own wives"* (Ephesians 5:28), and John says, *"We also ought to love one another"* (1 John 4:11). Those are biblical commands, not issues of liberty. One cannot withhold love from a spouse or fellow Christians while still glorifying God. When Paul tells us that a man *"ought not to have his head covered"* (1 Corinthians 11:7) and that *"the woman ought to have a symbol of authority on her head"* (1 Corinthians 11:10), he is speaking of something we need to do, not something we can choose if we want to do.

What Difference Does It Make?

Having made a case for why head covering should be understood as a command, let's now look at what difference this makes. What do we mean (and not mean) when we call something a command?

Being a biblical command
- does not mean you cannot disagree with the interpretation (and thus not observe it).
- does not mean it must be enforced by another (although this may be perfectly acceptable, depending on the circumstance, i.e. a pastor over his congregation).

Having said that, there are some important differences for how we interact with a command in contrast to an issue of Christian liberty.

Being a biblical command
- means if you are convinced that it's being interpreted correctly, you are obligated to observe it.
- means you can persuade and exhort others to

observe it without being legalistic.

I understand that calling this a command may be uncomfortable to some who read this. After all, aren't we under grace and freed from the Law? I am not suggesting a return to the old written code, which we have been released from (Romans 7:6). However, I am emphatically stating that Christianity is not a religion of lawlessness (Matthew 7:23). Paul said that we are under the *"law of Christ"* (1 Corinthians 9:21), and Jesus said, *"If you love Me, you will keep My commandments"* (John 14:15). That means Christianity and commandments are not antithetical.

Although head covering was taught by Paul (not Jesus), we are told that *"All Scripture is inspired by God"* (2 Timothy 3:16), and the apostle Peter considered Paul's writings to be Scripture too (2 Peter 3:15–16). That means the black letters are no less inspired than the red. Since 1 Corinthians 11 is authored by God, believers must study this passage with the same vigor they do with the rest of the Scriptures. If they are convinced that a cloth covering is in view and that it is a timeless symbol, they are obligated to observe it and can teach and exhort others to do the same.

Summary: A Biblical Case for Modern Head Covering

I appreciate you considering the positive case that I have made for head covering as a timeless and transcultural symbol. Some of you may be convinced and only have questions about practical application. Others still have objections, which we will be addressing over the next few chapters. Before we move on though, I think it would be helpful to review the main points we've covered so far.

Apostolic Tradition

"I praise you because you remember me in everything and hold firmly to the traditions, just as I delivered them to you." (1 Corinthians 11:2)

The word "traditions" in this context refers to teaching that comes from God, rather than from men. We examined the sentence structure and determined that head covering was one of these practices. This means that head covering during worship is apostolic teaching which was intended for us to "hold firmly" to.

Creation Order

"Christ is the head of every man, and the man is the head of a woman, and God is the head of Christ." (1 Corinthians 11:3)

"For a man ought not to have his head covered, since he is the image and glory of God; but the woman is the glory of man. For man does not originate from woman, but woman from man; for indeed man was not created for the woman's sake, but woman for the man's sake. Therefore the woman ought to have a symbol of authority on her head." (1 Corinthians 11:7–10a)

Head covering is a symbol that reflects the order of authority founded in the pre-Fall creation. The man with his uncovered head visibly shows that he possesses spiritual headship; whereas the woman with her covered head shows that she has submits to a man as her spiritual head. When Paul points back to Genesis as a reason why we must practice head covering, he turns all cultural arguments on their heads.

Angels

"Therefore the woman ought to have a symbol of authority on her head, because of the angels." (1 Corinthians 11:10)

Head covering is not just a symbol for the gathered church, but for the angels too. Since we do it for them, it presupposes that they either join us in worship or at least watch. Though we cannot know for certain everything that Paul meant by this verse, we can safely narrow it down to a few options. It could be 1) an appeal to not offend the angels by our disobedience, or 2) a command to accurately show them a picture of the created order (Ephesians 3:10; 1 Peter 3:22), or 3) a warning to us as a means of accountability (1 Timothy 5:21). Paul shows us in this verse that his concern is not what society thinks, but what the angelic beings think.

Nature

"Does not even nature itself teach you that if a man has long hair, it is a dishonor to him, but if a woman has long hair, it is a glory to her? For her hair is given to her for a covering." (1 Corinthians 11:14–15)

While head covering is taught explicitly in Scripture, it is confirmed by what nature silently teaches us as well. Nature shows us that the hair given to each sex confirms the appropriateness of head covering as they are in line with each other. It also teaches us that it is dishonorable when we disregard a gender distinction. So just as it is inappropriate to do that with our hair lengths, so it is with head covering while "praying and prophesying."

Church Practice

"*If anyone is inclined to be contentious, we have no such practice, nor do the churches of God.*" (1 Corinthians 11:16 ESV)

Paul tells us that among all the churches, none have the practice of women praying uncovered. When Paul wrote 1 Corinthians, these assemblies were spread out geographically over thousands of miles in many different countries and cultures. Despite this, they had a uniform practice of head covering. This shows that this was a universal Christian symbol rather than one of a specific culture.

Prescriptive

Issues that are Christian liberty are not commanded by God, and they allow for us to hold contrary positions while still glorifying Him (Rom 14:2–6). We took a look at the structure of 1 Corinthians 11 and laid out five reasons why head covering does not fit that description. This means that this teaching is a command that needs to be practiced. We also saw that when Paul said that the woman "*ought to have a symbol of authority on her head*" (1 Corinthians 11:10) that the word "ought" indicates obligation.

I hope this summary has been a helpful refresher of the main points we have covered. I would like to now transition to dealing with three of the most common objections to this practice.

SECTION TWO

OBJECTIONS TO HEAD COVERING

CHAPTER EIGHT

Long Hair: Our Natural Covering as the Only Covering?

"Verse 15 has been greatly misunderstood by many. Some have suggested that since a woman's 'hair is given to her for a covering,' it is not necessary for her to have any other covering. But such a teaching does grave violence to this portion of Scripture. Unless one sees that two coverings are mentioned in this chapter, the passage becomes hopelessly confusing."[48]
William MacDonald, president, Emmaus Bible College, 1959–65; author of *Believer's Bible Commentary*

The view that a head covering refers to a woman's long hair is a popular belief held by many Christians today. It comes from 1 Corinthians 11:14–15, which says:

"Does not even nature itself teach you that if a man has long hair, it is a dishonor to him, but if a woman has long hair, it is a glory to her? For her hair is given

---

48. William MacDonald, *Believer's Bible Commentary* (Thomas Nelson, 1995), 1786.

to her for a covering." (1 Corinthians 11:14–15)

Now, no one disputes that in these two verses Paul is talking about hair lengths. That is clear. Men are to have short hair, and women are to keep theirs longer. What is debated is how this passage relates to the rest of Paul's argument about covering. As discussed in chapter 4, this passage appeals to what nature teaches us about our hair lengths as a reason for why women should use an artificial covering. However, those who take the "long hair" view say that this is not a reason but an explanatory passage on what the covering is. It shows that Paul was concerned with hair lengths all along. Let's take some time to examine their arguments.

Fabricless Passage

One of the primary arguments for the "long hair" view is that nowhere in 1 Corinthians 11 does Paul tell women to wear an artificial covering. They point out that the word "veil" is not used here. That's true, since Paul tells women to cover their heads without ever telling them what to use as the covering. So the argument is, as per verse 15, that a woman's "long hair" is what will be a covering for her.

Before I respond to this claim, let's first take a historical look at this interpretation to see what the church has believed about this topic throughout the ages.

A New Interpretation

A. Philip Brown II (PhD, Bob Jones University) is one of the more prominent and articulate defenders of the "long hair" view. He says:

> *"On the whole, modern interpreters deviated little from identifying the covering Paul requires as a veil or material headdress until the mid-twentieth century.*

Although the view that the covering Paul required or forbade was itself long hair had been held popularly by various groups throughout the 20th century, Abel Isaakson [in 1965] was the first to offer the scholarly community an extended argument for this position in print." [49]

So Dr. Brown identifies the starting point of this view (which he holds himself) as the twentieth century. I was able to trace the view back a little further to the late nineteenth century,[50] but the point is, the "long hair" view is a new doctrine. It's different from how the church has understood this passage for nineteen hundred years. While church history is not the final authority, we should always be careful with brand-new views. As the old adage goes, *"If it's new, it's probably not true."*

The attestation to the head covering being an actual veil is very early. Irenaeus (AD 130–220) was an early Christian bishop and apologist. He was a disciple of Polycarp, who was a disciple of the apostle John. Irenaeus quotes 1 Corinthians 11:10 as *"A woman ought to have a veil upon her head, because of the angels."* [51] Notice he says "veil" instead of "authority." That shows us that Irenaeus understood this section of Scripture to refer to a fabric covering, not a woman's long hair. It should also be noted that Irenaeus

---

49. A. Philip Brown II, A Survey of the History of the Interpretation of 1 Corinthians 11:2–16 (Aldersgate Forum, 2011) Page 12.

50. The earliest advocate I could find was Karl Christian Johann Holsten (1825–1897), a German liberal theologian. More info at http://www.headcoveringmovement.com/articles/where-did-the-long-hair-view-come-from.

51. Irenaeus of Lyons, "Irenæus against Heresies" in *The Apostolic Fathers with Justin Martyr and Irenaeus*, vol. 1, ed. A. Roberts, J. Donaldson, and A. C. Coxe (Buffalo: Christian Literature Company), 327.

was a Roman citizen and a native Greek speaker (the language Paul wrote in). So he would be less likely to misunderstand Paul's choice of words since this was his native area and language.

Other notable church fathers who said that a fabric head covering was what Paul commanded include: Clement of Alexandria (AD 150–215), Hippolytus (AD 170–236), Tertullian (approx. AD 155–220), John Chrysostom (AD 347–407), Jerome (AD 347–420) and Augustine (AD 354–430). [52]

Greek Usage

In 1 Corinthians 11, the apostle Paul uses a few different words to refer to one's head being covered or uncovered. Please follow me as we do a study on these words. It will be a little more technical, but I think you will find it beneficial. I am going show you how the Greek words Paul uses for "covering" and "uncovering" are used in other writings. That is how scholars determine what ancient words mean.

You could just look up the word in a Greek lexicon (a dictionary for Greek words) and it will state what a word means. But I want to show you how the lexicons come up with their definitions. So we'll now transition to looking at relevant usage of these words in other Greek writings. By relevant I mean they need to be speaking about a covering for the "head" and they also need to have been written close to when the apostle Paul penned his letter (approximately AD 54). That criteria is important since words change meaning over time.

Kata Kephalē Echōn

The Greek words translated *"something on his head"* in 1

---

52. To read these quotations, please see Chapter 1 "A History of Christian Head Covering."

Corinthians 11:4 is *kata kephalē echōn*. *Kata* is a preposition that likely indicates a downward direction. It is not translated in the NASB, but instead they add the word "something" to show its broad scope. *Kephalē* is a noun, and it's rendered as "head." Finally, *echōn* is a verb that means "having," and it's rendered in this translation as "his." The way we can determine what Paul meant by the phrase is by seeing how it is used elsewhere. Now, these words appear only here in the New Testament, but there are two other relevant instances that we should take into consideration.

The first usage is in the Septuagint, which is the Greek translation of the Old Testament. This was the Bible used by the apostles. In Esther 6:12 it says, "*But Haman hurried to his house, mourning and with his* head covered." The words translated "head covered" is *kata kephalē* in Greek. Those are the words used in 1 Corinthians 11:4. This is a passage that obviously refers to a material head covering because you can't grow long hair while you're running home.

Another notable use of these words is by Plutarch, who was a Greek historian and Roman citizen. He also lived during the same years that Paul wrote his letters. Plutarch, writing about a man with a toga on his head, said: "*He was walking having his toga covering his head [kata kephalē echōn]*" (Regum 82.13). This is the exact same phrasing Paul used in 1 Corinthians 11. The fact that Plutarch was a contemporary of Paul, living in the same region and speaking the same language, means that the way he used words is very helpful for comparison. When Plutarch wanted to speak about a material head covering, he used *kata kephalē echōn* to describe it.

Katakalyptō and *Akatakalyptos*

While *kata kephalē* is only used once in the head covering passage, the words *katakalyptō* (covering) and *akatakalyptos* (uncovering) are used a total of five times. This is the same word, but the latter is in the negative form. Let's also take a brief look at how those words are used elsewhere.

Both of these words only appear in the New Testament in 1 Corinthians 11. Outside the New Testament both words consistently refer to a material covering when used in reference to one's head. The *Theological Dictionary of the New Testament* confirms that *"outside the NT [katakalyptō] is found in the sense of 'to veil' or 'to veil oneself.'"* Let's now look at some of the relevant uses of these two words.

Plutarch (AD 46–120) uses *katakalyptō* to speak of a local marriage custom when he says:

> *"In Boeotia it is the custom, when they **veil** the virgin bride, to set upon her head a chaplet of wild asparagus."*

In the apocryphal book of Susanna, (1st–2nd century BC), *katakalyptō* is used to refer to her material covering. It says:

> *"Now Susanna was a woman of great refinement, and beautiful in appearance. As she was **veiled**, the wicked men ordered her to be unveiled, that they might feed upon her beauty."* (Susanna 31–32 RSV)

Philo (20 BC–AD 50) speaking about a woman accused of adultery says:

> *"And the priest shall take the barley and offer it to the woman, and shall take away from her the head-dress on her head, that she may be judged with her head bare, and deprived of the symbol of modesty, which all those women are accustomed to wear who are completely blameless."* (*Special Laws*, III, 56)

Then he continues a few paragraphs later:

> *"when all these things are previously prepared, the woman with her **head uncovered [akatakalyptō tē kephalē]**, bearing the barley flour in her hand, as has*

been already specified, shall come forward." (*Special Laws*, III, 60)

The Greek words used for "head uncovered" are *akatakalyptō tē kephalē*, which is Paul's exact word choice in 1 Corinthians 11:5.

Just so there's no misunderstanding, *katakalypto* by itself does not exclusively refer to veils. Much like the English verb "cover," it requires context to know what is meant. To show you a range of uses, in the Septuagint *katakalypto* describes water covering the sea (Habakkuk 2:14), fat that covers parts of an animal (Leviticus 4:8), and words that are concealed (Daniel 12:9). However, when *katakalypto* or *akatakalyptos* are used to refer to the human head, it always refers to a material covering. Every single time.[53] Since that is the case, it is clear that when Paul spoke of *kata kephalē*, *katakalyptō*, or *akatakalyptos*, his readers would have understood him as referring to a fabric covering, not one's own hair.

Peribolaion

We have looked at five of the six references for "cover" and "uncover." And we saw that when Paul refers to "covering," he calls it *kata kephalē* or *katakalypto* and "uncovering"

---

53. In Isaiah 6:2 where we read about angels in heaven. It says the *"seraphim stood above Him, each having six wings: with two he covered his face, and with two he covered his feet, and with two he flew."*

In this passage we see that the seraphim use their wings as a covering for their face. The word used for "covered" in the Septuagint is *katakalypto*. Even though this does not refer to a material covering, it does refer to a removable veiling. The angels can move their wings in front or away from their face at will to veil or unveil. It is also a unique instance since it refers to angels in heaven rather than humans here on earth.

akatakalyptos. Now let's look at the last Greek word translated "covering," which comes from verse 15.

> *"Does not even nature itself teach you that if a man has long hair, it is a dishonor to him, but if a woman has long hair, it is a glory to her? For her hair is given to her for a **covering [peribolaion]**."* (1 Corinthians 11:14–15)

In the one passage that actually speaks about a woman's long hair, Paul differentiates between this and the covering called for in the rest of the chapter by using a completely different Greek word. In the one verse where he is clearly talking about hair, he calls the covering a *peribolaion*, whereas in the rest of the chapter when he talks about how women are to worship he uses *katakalypto*. So if verse 15 was an explanatory verse and Paul was actually talking about hair lengths all along, wouldn't he have called a woman's long hair *katakalypto*?

Some object that the reason for the difference is because *peribolaion* is the first instance in this passage where "covering" is referred to as a noun. While this grammar usage is true, it should be noted that *peribolaion* is from a completely different word group. If Paul was referring to the same covering and wanted to mention the noun form he likely would have called it *kalymma*. That is the noun form of the same word group, and Paul himself uses this word in another one of his letters to refer to a veil (see 2 Corinthians 3:12–16).

So even though English versions of the Bible translate both words as covering, Paul differentiates between the two coverings by using different Greek words.

Instead of a Covering?

The second major argument for the long hair view comes

from the word *anti* in Greek. In 1 Corinthians 11:15 this is translated as the word "for" where it says *"her hair is given to her* for *a covering."* The argument is that "for" is a poor translation and it should be rendered as *"in place of."* So they would interpret this passage as saying that a woman's hair is given to her *instead of* a fabric head covering. Meaning, if she has long hair, she needs nothing else. While it is true that the preposition *anti* can refer to substitution, this is not its exclusive meaning. The Greek lexicon BDAG indicates that "anti" has various types of meanings *"from replacement to equivalence."*

Dr. Thomas Schreiner, professor of New Testament Interpretation, Southern Baptist Theological Seminary, affirms,

> *"The preposition anti in 11:15 need not refer to substitution. It can also indicate equivalence. The latter makes better sense in the context."*

To prove that this is true, let me show you a few other examples where *anti* does not refer to substitution:

John 1:16 says, *"For from his fullness we have all received, grace **upon [anti]** grace"* (ESV).

In Acts 12:23 Luke says. *"Immediately an angel of the Lord struck him **because [anti hos]** he did not give God the glory."*

Finally, in 1 Thessalonians 5:15, Paul says, *"See that no one repays anyone evil **for [anti]** evil"* (ESV).

In each of the three examples put forth, *anti* is not used to indicate substitution.

Now that we've reviewed the major arguments for the "long hair" view, let's turn our attention to some additional reasons why I see two distinct coverings in this passage.

Short Hair Being Cut Short

If long hair is the only covering mentioned in this chapter, then verse 6 has a major problem. Let me show you what I mean.

If long hair was the same as being covered according to Paul, what would uncovered mean? It would mean having short hair, right? The opposite of covered is uncovered, and the opposite of long hair is short hair. So if that's what Paul had in mind, let's do some word replacement in verse 6. Where we see the word "cover her head," let's replace that with "have long hair."

> *"For if a woman does not [have long hair], let her also have her hair cut off."* (1 Corinthians 11:6)

Let's look at it again in another Bible translation.

> *"For if a wife will not [have long hair], then she should cut her hair short."* (1 Corinthians 11:6 ESV)

If a woman refuses to have long hair, she should cut her hair short? But she would already have short hair! This argument does not make any sense. Paul must be talking about an artificial covering.

Some then object to the ESV rendering of "cut short." They would understand "cut off" (NASB) as a synonym for shaved, making this argument less nonsensical. Paul's argument would then be transformed into "if a woman has short hair, she should shave it all off." The problem with this argument is that "cut off" cannot mean shaved in this context.

The Greek word translated "cut off" is *keirō*. This word is used again later in this very same passage, and it's differentiated from "shaved," which is the Greek word *xuraō*.

Here's what it says: *"but if is disgraceful for a woman to have her hair cut off [keirō] or her head shaved [xuraō]."* Did you catch it? He said "or" shaved. So while "cut off" [*keirō*] can be used to describe a shaved head, Paul could not have had this in mind here. If we were to understand it that way, his argument becomes *"if it is disgraceful for a woman to have her hair [shaved] or her head shaved."* Shaved or shaved? Once again that just would not make sense.

Not All the Time

Paul is concerned with covering only during specific times. He says:

> *"Every man who has something on his head while praying or prophesying disgraces his head. But every woman who has her head uncovered while praying or prophesying disgraces her head."* (1 Corinthians 11:4–5)

He makes it clear he is not talking about what happens all the time, but he is talking about what happens at a specific time. This is about what one wears on their head when engaged in acts of worship. So the very fact he limits the covering to specific times hints that he has a removable covering in mind. This is something you can put on and take off, not what is permanent like our hair.

Veiled Glory

In verse 15 a woman's long hair is called her glory, whereas earlier, in verse 10, Paul says a woman is to wear a "symbol of authority" on her head. The fact that these two purposes are antithetical shows us more than one covering is being discussed. Long hair is a woman's glory, whereas a head covering veils glory and is a symbol of authority. Those are not the same thing.

Greek scholar Dr. Daniel Wallace says about this point: *"Verses 10 and 15 would have to be saying the same thing if long hair is the same as a head covering. But this can hardly be the case. In v. 10, a woman is required to wear a 'symbol of authority.' Such a symbol represents her submission, not her glory . . . A literal translation would be: 'it is a glory to her' or 'a glory accruing to her,' or 'to her advantage.' Surely this is not the point of v. 10!"* [54]

Conclusion

While we affirm that a woman's long hair is her natural covering, we see two different coverings being talked about in this chapter. One of them is her hair, which is natural, permanent, and a glory to her (1 Corinthians 11:14–15). The other would be a fabric covering, which is artificial, removable (1 Corinthians 11:5), and a symbol of authority (1 Corinthians 11:10). A woman is to wear the latter when "praying and prophesying."

---

[54] Wallace, "What is the Head Covering in 1 Cor 11:2-16 and Does it Apply to Us Today?" https://bible.org/article/what-head-covering-1-cor-112-16-and-does-it-apply-us-today, accessed April 27, 2016

CHAPTER NINE

Culture: Harlotry, Roman Marriage, and a Localized Situation

"Every reason that Paul gives for the head covering is not cultural and yet evangelicals frequently say, 'oh well, that's a cultural thing; we don't have to pay any attention to it.' The reasons are not cultural. Creation. Woman's hair itself. Nature itself. Angelic beings are looking down upon us. Those are not cultural reasons." [55]
Dr. S. Lewis Johnson Jr., professor at Dallas Theological Seminary for 30+ years; pastor for 50+ years

The most popular objection against the practice of head covering is that Paul's instructions were only about a local situation. This suggests his intention was not that every church would have women covering their heads, but, rather, only those that had the same local customs as Corinth. Some speculate that in Paul's day, only prostitutes wore their hair short and did not cover their heads. Others

---

55. S. Lewis Johnson, "Covering the Head in Worship," accessed at http://sljinstitute.net/pauls-epistles/1corinthians/covering-the-head-in-worship.

proclaim that a head covering was the sign of a faithful married woman in Roman culture. Since the situation was local, they conclude that a head covering is not necessary today.

While looking at the culture of the time can often be helpful, it becomes dangerous when we start assigning reasons for a command that are different than what the author gives.

Dr. R.C. Sproul Sr. says,

"If Paul merely told women in Corinth to cover their heads and gave no rationale for such instruction, we would be strongly inclined to supply it via our cultural knowledge. In this case, however, Paul provides a rationale which is based on an appeal to creation not to the custom of Corinthian harlots." [56]

He goes on to say,

"We must be careful not to let our zeal for knowledge of the culture obscure what is actually said." [57]

In 1 Corinthians 11 Paul appeals to the creation order, nature's witness, and angels, all which transcend culture. He tells us that head covering is a part of official apostolic teaching and is the practice of all churches everywhere. So that means a local situation in Corinth cannot explain head covering, since it was the standard practice outside Corinth as well. Earlier in Paul's letter when he issued a command because of the situation at the time, he mentioned it. He recommended not to marry *"in view of the present distress"* (1 Corinthians 7:26). Paul could have done the same with the issue of head covering, but he didn't because what was happening at the time was not the reason for the command. Additionally, the fact that he commands men to remove their coverings in the same sentence cannot be explained by a situation that deals only with women.

---

56. R.C. Sproul, *Knowing Scripture* (Downers Grove, Illinois: InterVarsity Press, 1977), 110.

57. Ibid.

One Thousand Cult Prostitutes

In addition to exegetical grounds, there are also solid historical reasons for rejecting a cultural explanation of head covering. As mentioned, some believe that a woman with a bare head meant that she was advertising herself as a prostitute. The most appealed-to reference in support of this position is the one thousand cult prostitutes at the temple of Aphrodite in Corinth.

Before we examine that claim, we need a brief history lesson on the city of Corinth. Dr. Dirk Jongkind (Cambridge University) says, *"The City of Corinth had a glorious Hellenic past before its destruction by the Romans in 146 BC. Yet when it was refounded in 44 BC, it was not rebuilt as a Greek city, but as a Roman colony."* [58]

So Greek Corinth had been destroyed, and it was rebuilt one hundred years later as a Roman colony. It was another hundred years after that when Paul wrote the letter of 1 Corinthians.

The primary source quoted to learn about these cult prostitutes is the Greek geographer Strabo (64/63 BC–AD 24). Strabo traveled widely and recorded what he saw, as we read in his work *Geographica*:

"And the temple of Aphrodite was so rich that it owned more than a thousand temple slaves, courtesans, whom both men and women had dedicated to the goddess." [59]

Take note of the past tense of the quote. Strabo wrote this about thirty years before Paul wrote 1 Corinthians.

---

58. Dirk Jongkind, "Corinth In The First Century AD: The Search for Another Class," Tyndale Bulletin 52.1, 139.

59. Strabo, *Geographica*, Book 8, Chapter 6, accessed May 1, 2016, on http://penelope.uchicago.edu/Thayer/E/Roman/Texts/Strabo/8F*.html.

Strabo was referring not to his present time, but to ancient times in Corinth's past. He later stated, *"The city of the Corinthians, then, was always great and wealthy."*[60] The key words are "then" and "was." In sharp contrast, in his day he saw on the summit *"a small temple of Aphrodite,"*[61] not the *"temple of Aphrodite [that] was so rich that it owned more than a thousand temple slaves."*[62]

Dr. David W. J. Gill (University of Oxford) writing on "The Importance of Roman Portraiture for Head-Coverings in 1 Corinthians 11:2–16" says:

> *"Some have taken the urge for women to wear veils as Paul ensuring that they were not mistaken for prostitutes or hetairai. Part of the reason for this view lies in the interpretation of Corinth as a 'sex-obsessed' city with prostitutes freely roaming the street. The 1,000 hetairai linked to the cult of Aphrodite, and the corresponding notoriety of Corinth, belong to the Hellenistic city swept away by Mummius in 146 BC. In contrast, the Roman shrine was far more modest."*[63]

Dr. Gill agrees that Corinth did have a wild sex-obsessed reputation and one thousand cult prostitutes in the temple of Aphrodite. However, that belonged to Greek Corinth, which was destroyed about two hundred years before Paul wrote 1 Corinthians.

Mistaken Identity

Some have refrained from making the connection to prostitution but instead say that a head covering indicated

---

60. Ibid., 204.

61. Ibid., 193.

62. Ibid., 191.

63. David W. J. Gill, "The Importance of Roman Portraiture for Head-Coverings in 1 Corinthians 11:2–16," Tyndale Bulletin 41.2.

that a woman was faithful, modest, and married. They argue[64] that a respectable woman would never appear in public without a veil over her head. However, this claim is contrary to archaeological evidence. Dr. David W. J. Gill once again explains:

"Public marble portraits of women at Corinth, presumably members of wealthy and prestigious families are most frequently shown bare-headed. This would suggest that it was socially acceptable in a Roman colony for women to be seen bare-headed in public."[65]

Dr. Cynthia L. Thompson (Yale) writing about archaeological evidence in Roman Corinth says:

"Because most of the women's portraits presented here portray women with uncovered heads, one may infer that bareheadedness in itself was not a sign of a socially disapproved lifestyle."[66]

Finally, Dr. Kelly Olson (University of Chicago), who wrote the book *Dress and the Roman Woman*, writes,

"The vast majority of female portrait busts we possess show the woman with an unveiled head, probably in order to display her elaborate hairstyle to the viewer."[67]

As they point out, the archaeological evidence supports the fact that is was normal for women be seen bareheaded. This isn't an isolated piece of evidence but what is "most

---

64. The most scholarly defense of this view comes from Bruce Winter in his book *Roman Wives, Roman Widows*. I have written a few critiques of this book, which you can find at www.headcoveringmovement.com/articles-series.

65. Ibid.

66. Cynthia L. Thompson, "Hairstyles, Head-coverings, and St. Paul: Portraits from Roman Corinth," *Biblical Archaeologist*, June 1988, 112.

67. Kelly Olson, *Dress and the Roman Woman* (New York: Routledge, 2008), 34.

frequently shown."

What about Men?

Since the apostle Paul also commands men to remove their head covering when praying or prophesying (1 Corinthians 11:4), let's also see if men having something on their heads would be culturally out-of-step. Dr. Richard E. Oster Jr. (Princeton Theological Seminary), writing on the "Use, Misuse and Neglect of Archaeological Evidence in Some Modern Works on 1 Corinthians," says:

"This Roman custom [of male liturgical head covering] can be documented for several generations before and after the advent of Christianity in Corinth. This custom is clearly portrayed on coins, statues, and architectural monuments from around the Mediterranean Basin."[68]

Dr. Oster is saying that men covering their heads during this time in (non-Christian) worship has strong archaeological support. Since Paul instructs the men to go against a common cultural practice, the cultural explanation must be rejected. Dr. Oster then concludes:

"The practice of men covering their heads in the context of prayer and prophecy was a common pattern of Roman piety and widespread during the late Republic and early Empire. Since Corinth was itself a Roman colony, there should be little doubt that this aspect of Roman religious practice deserves greater attention by commentators than it has received."[69]

Paul also called long hair on men "dishonorable" (1

---

68. Richard E. Oster Jr. "Use, Misuse and Neglect of Archaeological Evidence in Some Modern Works on 1 Corinthians" in *Zeitschrift für die Neutestamentliche Wissenschaft und die Kunde der Älteren Kirche*, vol. 83, issue 1–2 (published online 10.1515/zntw.1992.83.1-2.52, October 2009) 52–73.

69. Ibid.

Corinthians 11:14). Those who advocate a cultural view of hair lengths assume that long hair on men would have been seen as shameful in Paul's day. However, there is that solid literary evidence that suggests otherwise. Dr. Cynthia L. Thompson quotes Dio Chrysostom (AD 40–115) to show that there were notable exceptions to men wearing their hair short. She says:

> *"Paul was in harmony with general Greco-Roman customs as observed in iconography. His argument that 'nature,' with its universal implications, teaches men to have short hair, however, ignores important exceptions that, as a Roman citizen with claims to literacy in Greek, should have been known to him. Philosophers, priests, peasants, and barbarians are mentioned as exceptions to the rule of men's short hair by Dio Chrysostom, who criticizes philosophers for making a connection between their long hair and moral superiority: 'I still maintain that long hair [koman] must not by any means be taken as a mark of virtue. For many human beings wear it long because of some deity; and farmers wear long hair, without ever having even heard the word philosophy; and, by Zeus, most barbarians also wear long hair, some for a covering and some because they believe it to be becoming. In none of these cases is a man subjected to odium or ridicule.'"*[70]

Chrysostom says that there were many men who wore their hair long and they were not *"subjected to odium (hatred) or ridicule."* That's another way of saying it was normal. Not only that, but they weren't doing so to rebel against society because they saw it as a *"mark of virtue."* This is really important because the cultural argument assumes that Paul's Corinth had a completely different view on these issues than the modern Western world. Their view

---

70. Thompson, "Hairstyles," 104.

is propagated by saying that if a man was seen with long hair in that culture, people would have dropped their jaws in shock at the public display of shamefulness. As we've seen, that picture just does not fit the evidence. Paul was talking about God's order, not Corinthian sentiment.

Cynthia Thompson seems to find this troubling by wrongfully assuming that something taught by "nature" would be universally practiced. I don't believe that we should be surprised when sinful men and women do what is right in their own eyes. Men and women regularly do the opposite of what both natural and special revelation[71] teach us.

Conclusion

Paul does not leave us in the dark as to why women are to cover their heads and men are to refrain. The fact that he says, *"for this reason"* (1 Corinthians 11:10 NKJV) means the answer will be found in exegesis, not cultural analysis. Having said that, when we do examine Roman cultural practices in that day we see that: 1) men did cover their heads in non-Christian worship, and 2) women being seen without a covering was not an outrage or an association with a socially disapproved lifestyle. Since cultural arguments for head covering must ignore Paul's own explanation, they should be rejected.

---

71. Natural revelation is the created universe (Romans 1:20), and special revelation is God speaking through words (Scriptures and prophecy).

CHAPTER TEN

Legalism: Majoring in the Minors and a Distraction from More Important Things

"Granted, 'Let her cover her head' (1 Corinthians 11:6) may not be as important as 'pour yourself out for the hungry' (Isaiah 58:10)—if you can call any part of God's Word unimportant. But I figure if the king tells you to go conquer the hinterlands one day, and tells you to shoe his horse the next day, you should do them both without slacking. He is the king."[72]

Andrée Seu Peterson (Senior Writer, *WORLD Magazine*)

The head covering passage (1 Corinthians 11:2–16) is often classified under the "obscure" category in Scripture. One theologian said, *"head covering here and the man of sin in II Thessalonians are two of the three most obscure passages in the New Testament."* But is that so? This section of Scripture is debatable, and there are good objections to the practice

---

72. Andrée Seu Peterson, "A symbol of glory," *WORLD Magazine*, 2007, http://www.worldmag.com/2007/06/a_symbol_of_glory, accessed April 27, 2016.

that require much thought and study. But obscure? A truly obscure verse is not expanded upon, explained or defended. The meaning cannot be easily discerned because of its vagueness. Good examples of obscure verses are 1 Corinthians 15:29 (baptism for the dead), 1 Timothy 2:15 (women saved through childbearing) and 1 Corinthians 11:10 (covering "because of the angels"). Even though there's an obscure verse in the head covering passage (1 Corinthians 11:10b), the section as a whole is not.

- An obscure passage would likely occupy only a verse or two. Head covering is taught in fifteen consecutive verses.
- An obscure passage would be mentioned, but not explained. With head covering Paul says, *"I want you to understand"* (1 Corinthians 11:3), and then unpacks the meaning of the symbol.
- An obscure passage would be commanded but with no reason as to why. With head covering Paul gives reasons for why we are to practice it, including the creation order (verses 3, 7–10), nature's witness (v.14–15), and angels (v.10). He tells us that head covering is a part of official apostolic teaching (v.2) and is the practice of all churches, everywhere (v.16).

Rather than being obscure, head covering is the most well-defended symbol in the New Testament. No other symbol in Scripture has more reasons for why one is to practice it nor is any other given such a lengthy defense.

Only Mentioned Once

A similar objection is that head covering is only mentioned once in the Bible. This is true. But how many times does something need to be mentioned in Scripture before we take it seriously? The answer has to be just once, because of who the Author is.

"All Scripture is breathed out by God and profitable for teaching, for reproof, for correction, and for training in righteousness, that the man of God may be competent, equipped for every good work." (2 Timothy 3:16–17 ESV)

All Scripture is profitable. Not some and not just things that are mentioned many times, but *all*. Not only that, but *"all Scripture is . . . profitable for teaching."* This means that discussion and teaching on head covering is not a distraction but a proper response to belief in the inspiration of Scripture.

It is also worth noting that the apostle Paul devoted essentially the same amount of time to head covering as he did to the Lord's Supper. On both topics he felt the need to address them in only one of his letters. If repetition were to determine importance, then the apostle Paul saw head covering and the Lord's Supper as equally important. He would also see greeting one another with a holy kiss (which he mentioned four times) as more important than if women are able to be pastors (which he only mentioned once). Clearly, that is not the case.

Lesser Commands

Some think that prolonged discussion about this topic (and surely a movement dedicated to it) is distracting us from the more important commands like feeding the poor and sharing the gospel. First, are those commands more important than head covering? Well, yes. Yes, they are. I hope that doesn't surprise you. Head covering is far from the most important command. But, once again, we believe God is the Author of *"all Scripture"* and so all Scripture deserves to be taken seriously.

Let's take a look at how Jesus handled "lesser commands".

> *"Woe to you, scribes and Pharisees, hypocrites! For you tithe mint and dill and cumin, and have neglected the weightier matters of the law: justice and mercy and faithfulness. These you ought to have done, without neglecting the others."* (Matthew 23:23 ESV)

Jesus tells the Pharisees that tithing is not as important as justice, mercy, and faithfulness. The Pharisees got the small stuff right, but they neglected the more important commands. How did Jesus respond? He sharply rebukes them and tells them to start doing the *"weightier matters of the law."* However, He doesn't tell them to stop doing the less important commands. He wants them to do both. He tells them, *"These you ought to have done, without neglecting the others."*

In another instance when speaking about Old Testament laws, Jesus says:

> *"Therefore whoever relaxes one of the least of these commandments and teaches others to do the same will be called least in the kingdom of heaven, but whoever does them and teaches them will be called great in the kingdom of heaven."* (Matthew 5:19 ESV)

As we can see, Jesus didn't view lesser commands as optional. The least are to be observed along with the greatest. They need to be distinguished and kept in their proper places, but both are to be observed.

Legalism

Many who practice head covering today are viewed as legalistic. In order to comment on this charge, it is important to first define the term. The word "legalism" isn't found anywhere in the Bible, nor is anyone in the Scriptures referred to as "legalistic." It is a word coined to refer to an incorrect view of law-keeping. Generally speaking, when someone is legalistic they are doing one of two things:

    1. They believe their law-keeping makes (or keeps)

them in a right standing with God.

2. They make laws out of issues that Christians have liberty to decide for themselves.

For the first definition, it is possible to be legalistic about any teaching in Scripture. Head covering should not be singled out, as no command is immune from this error. Anyone can think that one's obedience earns justifying favor with God, no matter the issue. But, let me be clear, this is a heretical view. No amount of good works or law-keeping can make us (or keep us) right with God. Our salvation is a free gift, based upon the perfect life and death of Jesus in our place. Faith in Christ is what saves us, not obedience to Christ. We obey God out of love for Him (John 14:15), not to be loved by Him. Therefore, one can practice head covering without being legalistic in this sense.

The last definition of legalism is turning issues of Christian liberty into commands. Head covering could only be legalistic in that sense if the practice itself was not commanded in Scripture. Let's review several reasons from chapter 7 regarding on why we believe this symbol is not Christian liberty:

1. Head covering is teaching that was "held firmly" by the church because it was delivered with apostolic authority (1 Corinthians 11:2). Liberty issues are left to the Christian, not delivered to the churches for them to hold to.

2. Paul tells anyone who would disagree with head covering that the churches have only one view, and that is their practice of it (1 Corinthians 11:16). Liberty issues are marked by multiple views, not an exclusive position.

3. The sentence structure commands an action: *"But since it is disgraceful for a wife to cut off her hair or shave her head, **let her cover her head**"* (1 Corinthians 11:6 ESV). Liberty issues are marked by the absence of a direct action-command.

4. Paul says to not practice head covering is dishonorable, disgraceful, and comparable to a woman having a shaved head (1 Corinthians 11:4–6). Liberty issues are marked by a plurality of choices that can bring glory to God (Romans 14:6), while Paul's choice of language suggests that in this instance only one choice can.
5. Paul defends head covering by appealing to the creation order, nature, and angels. Liberty issues are marked by their silence in the Scriptures, not by a defense.

Since head covering is not a symbol that people can choose if they want to obey, I don't believe this definition of legalism can apply. It would be like saying, *"It's legalistic for you to tell a new Christian she must be baptized."* That would be a misapplied charge since baptism is a command, not a practice you decide if you want to partake of or not. When one is exhorted to adhere to a scriptural command, that is not legalism; it is biblical Christianity.

Conclusion

The teaching of head covering is not wrapped in obscurity. The Bible provides a lengthy explanation with many reasons for why we are to practice it. Since this is so, it is unfair to compare this to those who build a doctrine from a verse out of context or a passing vague statement in the Bible. While it is only mentioned one time, once is enough because God is the Author. Furthermore, one can hold to head covering without assigning an importance level to it that the Bible does not give.

To set different biblical commands against each other is a false dichotomy. It's not head covering *or* feeding the poor; it's head covering *and* feeding the poor. One does not have to stop serving to study and practice this biblical teaching. Finally, while head covering can be practiced legalistically, the source of legalism would be in the heart of the one who practices it, not in the symbol itself.

SECTION THREE

PRACTICAL APPLICATION

CHAPTER ELEVEN

What Style of Head Covering Should Be Worn?

"Covering the head is a religious act, not fashion display. The covering is a Christian symbol that she is under authority. So whatever a woman uses to cover her head when she prays it should correspond to the meaning of the act."[73]
Alexander Strauch (former professor at *Colorado Christian University*, author of *Biblical Eldership* and *Men and Women, Equal Yet Different*)

A head covering in the context of 1 Corinthians 11 is a Christian symbol to be worn by women while praying and prophesying. Paul says this covering is a symbol of authority (1 Corinthians 11:10) and it's to be worn on her head (1 Corinthians 11:5–6), but he does not specify what is to go on the head. It is the result he commands, of having a head covered, not that women need to have a specific type of covering for their heads. We know this is the case

---

73. Alexander Strauch, "Littleton Bible Chapel Position Paper: 1 Corinthians 11:2–16,"
http://www.headcoveringmovement.com/Littleton-Bible-Chapel-Position-Paper-Head-Coverings.pdf, accessed May 1, 2016, 14.

because Paul provides us only with a verb, not a noun. So he gives us an action to perform (cover your head), not a specific object to wear (like put on a scarf). Let me give you an analogy to show the significance of this: If I said to you, "I want you to call me," I'd be telling you the action I want you to take. I just need you to call me, but there are many different ways you can fulfill that. You could use your cell phone; you could use a landline phone; or you could use Skype. By using the verb "call" I'm not specifying a particular device; I just want the action of you calling me. But, now in contrast, if I used a noun in addition to the verb by saying, "I want you to call me with your iPhone," my instructions would be more specific. By using the noun iPhone, I've taken away your freedom in choosing your own device since I told you what device to use. If you called me using Skype, or on a landline phone, you wouldn't be following my instructions as I gave them.

This is significant because this is exactly how Paul speaks in 1 Corinthians 11. He commands women to take the action of covering their heads without specifying any particular garment that should be used. So where Scripture ends, Christian liberty begins. That means the type of covering you use is your decision as an individual, family, or church. That also means that those who say a covering must be a certain style or it's not a true covering are going further than the Bible does. Because the grammar of this passage is clear, it's an action, not an object that is commanded.

Veiling the Glory of Man

Now, having said that, there's a helpful question women should ask themselves when selecting a covering. The Bible says that a woman is the glory of man and when she is worshiping the glory of man is to be veiled. The Greek word used for cover is *katakalyptō*, which means to veil, hide, or conceal. So when a woman covers her head, she's symbolically concealing the glory of man so that only God's glory is on display. Since the purpose of head covering is to hide human glory, it's important that a woman honestly ask herself, *"Is this head covering I've chosen portraying that or is just accentuating my own glory?"* See, some "coverings" may be better categorized as a hair accessories, which call attention to the hair, rather than a covering, which veils it. So I think it's important to remember the purpose of covering and to honestly ask yourself if the garment you've chosen is faithful to what it symbolizes.

Modesty and Discreetness

While there are no instructions regarding the type of covering one can use, there are a few principles we do need to take into consideration. Both the apostles Paul and Peter instructed women to dress modestly and discreetly, letting their internal adornment (not external) be what's on display. Here's what they said:

> *"Likewise, I want women to adorn themselves with proper clothing, modestly and discreetly, not with braided hair and gold or pearls or costly garments, but rather by means of good works, as is proper for women making a claim to godliness."* (1 Timothy 2:9–10)

> *"Your adornment must not be merely external— braiding the hair, and wearing gold jewelry, or putting on dresses; but let it be the hidden person of the heart, with the imperishable quality of a gentle and quiet spirit, which is precious in the sight of God."* (1 Peter 3:3–4)

So how should women apply these principles to the coverings they choose to wear? I believe the application would be for them to cover their heads with something that is not overtly ostentatious. Once again, head covering is supposed to veil human glory, not accentuate it. Modesty and discreetness *does not* mean frumpy or devoid of beauty, but it also does not call attention to itself. Although the application of these principles will look different in each believer's life, the important thing is we actually take them seriously by asking ourselves if what we wear is in keeping with the spirit of these commands.

Must All Hair Be Covered?

Another issue regards how much hair can be exposed outside the covering. Must all her hair be hidden, or can some still show? The passage we looked at in the previous section helps us answer this question.

In 1 Timothy 2:1 Paul starts a new section that teaches *"how one ought to conduct himself in the household of God"* (1 Timothy 3:15). So we're talking about church issues here. Now just a few verses into this new section, Paul exhorts women to dress modestly in church, with one of the applications of that principle being to not have "braided hair" (1 Timothy 2:9). Since Paul told us that women covered their heads in all churches (1 Corinthians 11:16), and he also instructs them about their hairstyles, we must conclude that some hair was exposed outside the covering. That's how we harmonize those two passages. If Paul meant that a woman must cover all of her hair, then his instructions about not having elaborately braided hair would be unnecessary. In that case, his command for head coverings would eliminate anyone appearing in the assembly with braided hair.

I think it's interesting that when we look at archaeological evidence of Roman women in the first century, we see that the coverings they used still left their hairstyle visible.[74] The most common type of head covering used in Corinth was where the woman would pull the mantle she wore around her body up over her head. To help you visualize this, it's like pulling your hoodie up on top of your head. When that type of covering is used, we can still see what type of hairstyle you have. Since it rests on top of your head and drapes back, the front and sides of your head remain visible. In fact, we have numerous statues where a woman's head is covered but you can still clearly see the cornrows from her braided hair. Therefore I don't see this as a contradiction that if Paul spoke about women's hairstyles they couldn't have worn head coverings. I think this wrongly assumes a specific type of covering that wouldn't show any hair. So the fact that Paul addressed hairstyles in the context of church worship means that head coverings where hair is still exposed had to be perfectly acceptable.

Face Veils?

Some Christians teach that the covering Paul advocates is a Middle Eastern style that covered the face. Now, those who make such claims do not believe that head covering is for today. Since that is so, you have to wonder if they say this to discourage the practice. After all, what Christian woman desires to wear a burka? We have already established that Paul is not speaking about any specific type of head covering. However, what is clear is that he's speaking about

---

74. Dr. Kelly Olson mentions that the "*palla* or mantle, drawn over the head when the woman was out of doors" is the "description is offered by several modern scholars as that of the everyday clothing of the Roman matron." *Dress and the Roman Woman*, 25.

To see a visual example, the "Large Herculaneum Woman" can be viewed at http://www.getty.edu/art/exhibitions/herculaneum_women/lg_w oman.html, accessed May 1, 2016.

a *head* covering. He uses the Greek word for *head*, and never once does he use the Greek word for *face* in this passage. So the claim that a woman must cover her face in order to be faithful to this passage is bogus. I also think that a face covering would directly contradict what is taught in 2 Corinthians 3:18:

> *"But we all, with unveiled face, beholding as in a mirror the glory of the Lord, are being transformed into the same image from glory to glory."*

In context he's contrasting the believer (who has an unveiled face) with Moses who *"used to put a veil over his face"* (2 Corinthians 3:13). From this passage we can make two observations.

1. Since Paul writes to the Corinthians and mentions "unveiled face" (*anakekalymmenō prosōpō*), we know he could have used that wording in 1 Corinthians 11. Instead, he only mentioned "uncovered heads" (*akatakalyptō tē kephalē*) since that is his concern.

2. If Paul required all women (or even just Corinthian women) to veil their faces he couldn't have said *"we all, with unveiled face"* because it wouldn't be true. Only men would have "unveiled faces," not all believers whom he's speaking about. And if one were to object that Paul means "unveiled" only in a metaphoric sense, it's still hard to imagine Paul would have said this since it would be far too ironic.

Now some have suggested that this style of head covering was common during Paul's time, but no such evidence exists. There is evidence of face-veiling in areas such as Tarsus, Arabia, and Syria,[75] but not in Roman Corinth. An archaeological survey shows that women in Corinth were either seen uncovered or with a covering that

---

75. Thompson, "Hairstyles," 113

drapes down over the head (but not the face).[76] Even if there was evidence for face-veiling in Corinth, that still would not change anything. We get our instructions from Paul, not the culture he lived in, and he never tells a woman that her face must be covered. It is the action of women covering their heads and men uncovering their heads that is to happen.

Conclusion

So, in summary, the choice of covering you use for your head is yours to make. It should be modest, and it should fulfill its purpose of actually covering your head. Whether it covers all your hair, or only some of it, that is completely up to you. The type doesn't matter, only that the head is covered.

---

76. See Thompson, "Hairstyles" and Gill, "Roman Portraiture."

CHAPTER TWELVE

Where Is This to Be Practiced: Church Gatherings or Everywhere?

"When you come to the house of God for corporate worship, how you conduct yourself matters. Paul argues for proper decorum in public worship according to His created order."[77]
The Reformation Heritage KJV Study Bible

The Scriptures tell us that head covering is required for women when praying or prophesying. These terms are likely used as a synecdoche, which is a figure of speech where part of something is used to refer to the whole. So when Paul says that we don't struggle against *"flesh and blood"* (Ephesians 6:12), we understand that he uses those terms to refer to people. In the same way when he talks about "praying and prophesying" (1 Corinthians 11:4–5) he's using that to refer to our corporate worship.

New Testament scholar Dr. Gordon Fee says of these terms:

"The two verbs 'pray and prophesy' make it certain that the problem has to do with the assembly at

---

77. *The Reformation Heritage KJV Study Bible* (Reformation Heritage Publishers, 2014), 1661.

worship . . . *the two verbs are neither exhaustive nor exclusive but representative.*"[78]

So it's not just that women are to cover (and men uncover) when we engage in prayer or something prophetic. But the same instructions would apply in singing, preaching, partaking of the Lord's Supper, or anything else we do corporately[79] in our worship of God.

You may be wondering why it would be dishonorable for a woman to pray uncovered at church (1 Corinthians 11:5) but then be perfectly acceptable in her private devotions. This is because symbols can take on meaning at specific times or when engaged in certain actions. Let me illustrate this by looking at the other symbol mentioned in this very same chapter.

When we partake of the Lord's Supper we're doing so in remembrance of Christ (1 Corinthians 11:25). The bread and wine take on a symbolic meaning when we eat and drink of it corporately. There is nothing unique about bread or wine, but during the church gathering they are given a special significance. Think about it like this: at home you may eat bread and drink wine in any manner. They are common elements that we use for nourishment. However, when the symbol is partaken of during a church service, we are to examine ourselves first (1 Corinthians 11:28), and the Lord threatens sickness and death if we eat and drink of it unworthily (1 Corinthians 11:29–30).

The serious consequences should tell us that at *this time* the symbol is set apart as holy. It's not like any other time that we eat or drink of it. Though they are common in one

---

78. Gordon Fee, *The First Epistle to the Corinthians* (Wm. B. Eerdmans Publishing, 2014), 558.

79. Corporate worship should not be seen as exclusive to the Sunday service. I have written about various other corporate gatherings such as prayer meetings and conferences at http://www.headcoveringmovement.com/articles/is-corporate-worship-limited-to-the-sunday-service.

setting, they are set apart and infused with symbolic meaning in another. When we leave church we can eat and drink without examining ourselves just as women can cover or uncover their heads as they please. When we are not gathered corporately, then bread, wine, and a covering for our heads fulfill their common functions. However, when we do gather together they are set apart and given symbolic meaning.

So we just established that symbols can mean something in one setting, but not in another. We have also defined "prayer and prophecy" as representative of our corporate worship. But I have yet to explain from Scripture why I believe Paul is only speaking about our public worship (not private). I believe there are three clues from the context that show this to be the case. Let's go over those now.

The Commending Link

When you look at the structure of 1 Corinthians 11, it's divided very neatly. Verse 2 states *"Now I praise you"* followed by teaching on a topic they were practicing (head covering). Then in verse 17 Paul contrasts his first statement by saying, *"I do not praise you,"* followed by teaching on two practices they were doing in a harmful way (the Lord's Supper and spiritual gifts [80]).

Now when we see a new section, this indicates we have a new topic. So what we need to ask ourselves is, "What connects the three topics Paul deals with in this section?" He had already praised them (1 Corinthians 1:4) and rebuked them for many issues such as divisions over leaders (1:18 through 4:21), sexual immorality, and lawsuits (chapters 5 and 6). So why the new section when he had already been dealing with issues of this sort? What separates these three issues from the other topics in his

---

80. Paul deals with the misuse of spiritual gifts in 1 Corinthians 12 through 14.

letter?

John Murray (professor, Westminster Theological Seminary 1930–66) explains the connection well:

"There is good reason for believing that the apostle is thinking of conduct in the public assemblies of the church of God and of worship exercises therein in verse 17, this is clearly the case, and verse 18 is confirmatory. But there is a distinct similarity between the terms of verse 17 and of verse 2. Verse 2 begins, 'Now I praise you,' and verse 17, 'Now in this . . . I praise you not.' The virtually identical expressions, the one positive and the other negative, would suggest, if not require, that both have in view the behavior of the saints in their assemblies."[81]

The reason why these three topics are linked together is because they all deal with issues pertaining to corporate worship. Verses 2 and 17 connect the topics together, and verse 18, *"when you come together as a church,"* clearly shows the context Paul is addressing.

Murray continues:

"If a radical difference, that between private and public, were contemplated, it would be difficult to maintain the appropriateness of the contrast between 'I praise you' and 'I praise you not.'"[82]

The Churches of God

A second reason why the local assembly is in view comes from the final verse on head covering, which states:

---

81. John Murray, "Head Coverings and Decorum in Worship: A Letter," Point 3, www.headcoveringmovement.com/articles/head-coverings-and-decorum-in-worship-a-letter-by-john-murray, accessed on April 27, 2016.

82. Ibid.

"If anyone is inclined to be contentious, we have no such practice, nor do the churches of God." (1 Corinthians 11:16)

In this verse Paul appeals to what the "churches of God" are doing. By calling attention to the uniform practice of these assemblies, he indicates that this is an assembly issue. He doesn't say it's the practice of all individual Christians, but rather of all local churches. As a parallel, when Paul uses similar language shortly after, it is clearly in reference to local assembly conduct: *"As in all the churches of the saints, the women should keep silent in the churches"* (1 Corinthians 14:33b–34 ESV).

New Testament Prophecy

A final clue that Paul has the local church in mind is that he says we are to practice this when we prophesy. This is important because prophecy in 1 Corinthians is a gift that edifies the church (1 Corinthians 14:4).

See, sometimes we know *where* we're talking about by *what* we're talking about. If I mention taking the Lord's Supper, do you the know setting I'm talking about? Of course! The Lord's Supper is to be eaten when we meet together as a church. It's not something you practice in private. Likewise, prophecy is something that is always done in public settings.

Now, granted, prophecy in the Bible is nuanced. There are authoritative proclamations that men like Isaiah gave on behalf of God, and there is musical prophecy like the sons of Asaph who *"were to prophesy with lyres, harps, and cymbals"* (1 Chronicles 25:1). Both of those types are also different from the prophecy mentioned in 1 Corinthians, which needs to be judged (14:29–31). That was never said about prophecy in the Old Testament. When a term doesn't have a uniform meaning, it's important to not stray from the context in taking our definition. If Paul wants women to cover their heads when they prophesy, we should allow him to give us the definition of prophecy, since that's what he has in mind. When we do that, we see that he's speaking about the time when *"the whole church assembles together"* (1 Corinthians 14:23–25).

Now that I've given you three clues from the context for why I believe the local assembly is in view, let's transition to dealing with the three main arguments against this position.

Praying without Ceasing

While prophecy is a public gift, prayer is clearly not. Prayer is something that we can do privately or even in our head. Since we are called to *"pray without ceasing"* (1 Thessalonians 5:17), why don't I believe that women must cover their heads virtually all the time? Let me answer that question by using another example from Scripture.

In 1 Timothy 2:12 Paul says, *"But I do not allow a woman to teach or exercise authority over a man."* In context, he is saying that women cannot teach the Scriptures to men in church (1 Timothy 3:14). So even though we see the word "teach," we understand that he's not speaking about all *types* of teaching in all *settings*. So we'd never say a woman can't "teach" a man how to read another language or how to use a computer program. We understand that the prohibited teaching is a certain *type*: biblical instruction. Neither is he forbidding women from teaching men theology in all *settings* since Priscilla helped to teach Apollos (a preacher) the Christian faith more accurately (Acts 18:26). So just as we don't see the word "teach" (1 Timothy 2:12) and apply it in the broadest terms possible, neither should we when we see the word "prayer" (1 Corinthians 11:4–5). We can acknowledge that, because of the context, Paul is speaking about prayer in a certain setting.

In The First Place

Some argue that when Paul says *"in the first place"* (1 Corinthians 11:18), the word "first" indicates a new setting (the local church). Therefore, it is argued that head covering shouldn't be understood as a church issue since it was dealt with before he said that.

Let's take a look at the verses in question together.

> *"But in giving this instruction, I do not praise you, because you come together not for the better but for the worse. For, in the first place, when you come together as a church, I hear that divisions exist among you; and in part I believe it."* (1 Corinthians 11:17–18)

Dr. John MacArthur (pastor and founder of *Grace To You*) best articulates this argument:

> *"Now people say about* [1 Corinthians 11:5], *'Well, wait a minute, here are women praying and prophesying. Isn't that in the church?' Well, it doesn't say so. Let me show you something. I think he's just talking about general things. I don't think he's talking about the formal worship of the church, the coming together of the church. You say, 'Why don't you?' Go down to verse 18, this is really the first time he gets into issues about the church. Look what it says. 'For first of all,' what is that again? Literally in the Greek, 'In the first place,' which means if this is the first place there isn't any place before this. If this is first of all, there isn't anything else related to what he's going to talk about. So, first of all, 'When you come together in the church,' may I suggest to you that nobody has come together in the church until that verse?"* [83]

Let me quickly clarify the context before we look at this

---

83. John MacArthur, "God's High Calling for Women, Part 3," accessed at http://www.gty.org/Resources/Sermons/54-16.

verse more closely. Paul had just concluded his teaching on head covering, a topic he had praised them for maintaining (1 Corinthians 11:2). In verse 17 he now switches to issues that he cannot praise them for, the first being their abuse of the Lord's Supper.

While it is possible to understand *"in the first place"* as referring to their coming *"together as a church,"* it is more likely that he is referring to the first issue that he could not praise them for. So it's Paul speaking of the "first" abuse rather than the "first" time he's dealing with an issue in this setting. See, if you were just told that when you gathered together as a church it's *"for the worse,"* you'd want to know why. And Paul does just that. He says the first way their meetings are *"for the worse"* is their divisions during the Lord's Supper. The second reason comes immediately after, when he says, *"Now concerning spiritual gifts"* (1 Corinthians 12:1).

Jamieson, Fausset, and Brown in their popular commentary say it this way:

> *"He does not follow up the expression, 'in the first place,' by 'in the second place.' But though not expressed, a second abuse was in his mind when he said, 'In the first place,' namely, the abuse of spiritual gifts, which also created disorder in their assemblies."*[84]

Women Must Be Silent

Another major argument against head covering being a church issue is that Paul later says, *"The women are to keep silent in the churches; for they are not permitted to speak"* (1 Corinthians 14:34). The argument is, if women cannot speak in the assembly, then Paul couldn't be instructing women how to pray and prophesy there. Therefore, it is concluded

---

84. R. Jamieson, A. R. Fausset, and D. Brown, *Commentary Critical and Explanatory on the Whole Bible*, vol. 2 (Oak Harbor, WA: Logos Research Systems, Inc., 1997), 284.

that he must be talking about other non-church settings.

While I understand the argument, I don't see Paul's command for women to be silent as a prohibition against all types of speech. Paul had just told the person who speaks in tongues (but doesn't have anyone to interpret) that he is to *"keep silent in church and speak to himself and to God"* (1 Corinthians 14:28). Notice, even though he is to *"keep silent"* he is also to *"speak to himself and to God."* So "silent" in that verse is not total, but is about speaking out loud in tongues. In the same way, women being *"silent in the churches"* is referring to how they are to receive instruction. Paul says that *"a woman must quietly receive instruction with entire submissiveness"* (1 Timothy 2:11), and *"if they desire to learn anything, let them ask their own husbands at home"* (1 Corinthians 14:35). So while women may pray, sing, and exercise spiritual gifts in church gatherings, they are forbidden from speaking up during instruction.

Summary

When Paul refers to prophecy, he expects it to be happening in a public setting. Though we do pray privately, it is also one of the primary things we are called to do corporately (1 Timothy 2:1–3). Because the context links this passage together with teaching that is explicitly for when the church is gathered together (1 Corinthians 11:17–18, 20, 33), it's best to understand Paul as having corporate practices in mind. His final appeal to what is practiced by all local assemblies (1 Corinthians 11:16) confirm that this is a church issue.

CHAPTER THIRTEEN

Should Girls and Single Women Wear Head Coverings Too?

"Is it only married women? This in my estimation is a common misunderstanding of the passage. It ends up orientating the passage toward marriage when in fact the passage is not making that kind of distinction at all."[85]
Dr. Mark Minnick, Professor of New Testament Studies and Church Ministries, Bob Jones University

In 1 Corinthians 11, Paul instructs women that they are to wear a head covering when "praying or prophesying." The Greek word behind "woman" is *gynē*, and it can be translated as "woman" or "wife" depending on the context. While almost all English versions of the Bible[86] translate *gynē* as "woman" in verses 2–16, the popular English Standard Version[87] differs by translating some of the

---

85. Mark Minnick, "Questions and Answers about Headcoverings," preached on June 14, 2015, at Mount Calvary Baptist Church, http://www.mountcalvarybaptist.org.
86. Examples include the NIV, NASB, KJV, NKJV, HCSB, and NET versions.
87. The RSV also advocates this view by translating 1

references as "wife." This has led many to wonder if head covering is only applicable for those who are married. Behind the ESV's translation decision [88] is an assumption that a woman wearing a head covering was a first-century Roman symbol of being a matron (respectable married woman). I will be arguing that Paul's teaching on head covering is for all men and women, regardless of their marital status.

Creation Order or Marriage Order?

As mentioned, the Greek word *gynē* can be translated as wife or woman depending on the context. Here are some example uses that refer to or include non-married women.

- John uses the word to refer to a Samaritan woman living with a man who is not her husband (John 4:17).
- Paul applies the word to both a betrothed and an unmarried woman (1 Corinthians 7:34).
- Paul also uses the word in teaching that women are to learn quietly in church—obviously not just those who are married (1 Timothy 2:11).

Since *gynē* can refer to unmarried women, the question that needs to be asked is: Is there anything in the context that indicates only married women are in view? For support, 1 Corinthians 11:3 is usually appealed to, which states:

"But I want you to understand that Christ is the head of every man, and the man is the head of a woman, and God is the head of Christ."

Corinthians 11:3 as "the head of a woman is her husband."

88. Wayne Grudem and Bruce Winter are two outspoken advocates of the cultural marriage view. They are two of the fourteen men who sit on the ESV Translation Oversight Committee.

The argument from this passage is that a woman only has one head, and that is her husband. While that is true, I believe the scope of Paul's argument is far broader than married individuals. In this passage of Scripture, Paul is stating the order of Creation, not the order of marriage roles. After all, every man has Christ as head, not just every husband. So this is not a limited statement that includes only a portion of people, but rather is an all-encompassing statement that relates to everyone. He is dealing with men and women and their roles as determined by Creation, not John and Jane as a couple. We know he has Creation roles in mind because he expands upon this in verses 7–9. Here's what he says there:

"For a man ought not to have his head covered, since he is the image and glory of God; but the woman is the glory of man. For man does not originate from woman, but woman from man; for indeed man was not created for the woman's sake, but woman for the man's sake."

We see here that Paul is talking about the big picture—the differences between men and women as a whole. Once again, he doesn't have a narrow focus of married individuals. If he did, and if we consistently translated *gynē* as wife here, we'd be left with Paul saying that wives originate from their husbands (1 Corinthians 11:8). This absurdity, although no one espouses it, forcefully makes the point that women (not just wives) are in view.

Dr. Daniel Wallace (Dallas Theological Seminary) is one of the leading conservative Greek scholars. In a paper he wrote on head covering, he agrees that there is no contextual reason to translate *gynē* as wife. He says:

"We have not discussed at all whether single women or married women are in view in this text . . . Suffice it to say that [gynē] should be taken as woman (as opposed to 'wife') unless there are sufficient contextual reasons

to argue otherwise."[89]

Mary Kassian (Professor of Women's Studies, SBTS) also sees women in view because of the universal relevance of Paul's arguments. Speaking of 1 Corinthians 11:13–15, she says:

> *"The hair length illustration used indicates that he thought the ruling applied to all. Otherwise, the illustration loses its force, since hair length applied to all women, not just married ones."*[90]

She then explains what head covering means to women who are not married:

> *"By wearing covering, a single women stated: 'I recognize that God has ordered women to submit within the marriage relationship. Even though I am not married, I understand this principle, and I show my respect for it by wearing a head covering. Even if I never marry, I wear a symbol which recognizes my place in creation.'"*[91]

Wedding Scenes and Worship Attire

While 1 Corinthians 11:3 is sometimes appealed to as a reason for seeing marital roles in view, the main reason for this understanding comes from Roman culture. Dr. Wayne Grudem (General Editor, *ESV Study Bible*), an advocate of the married view, says:

> *"Evidence that head covering for a woman indicated that she was married is found both in literary sources and in archeological discoveries of artwork portraying*

---

89. Wallace, "What is the Head Covering in 1 Cor 11:2-16 and Does it Apply to Us Today?" Footnote 8, https://bible.org/article/what-head-covering-1-cor-112-16-and-does-it-apply-us-today, accessed April 27, 2016. Dr. Wallace holds to the 'symbol replacement' view.

90. Kassian, *Women*, 100.

91. Ibid., 101.

wedding scenes."[92]

We must first point out that Grudem is looking in the wrong place for relevant evidence. He is looking to "wedding scenes" for support, but Paul is only concerned with how one worships. If one were to peer in on a twenty-first century North American "wedding scene" they would likely see the bride veiled as well. However, this snapshot would be inaccurate if it was used as evidence for how she worships, since she does not wear her bridal veil after her wedding. The *flammeum,* a distinct Roman marriage veil that was worn by the bride, was not worn after her wedding either.[93] So wedding scenes are unhelpful for Paul's discussion on worship attire.

The Roman Matron

It is often cited that in Roman culture any respectable married woman (or "matron") would not be seen in public without a covering over her head. This connection between a covered head and being a respectable married woman is seen by some as inseparable. Before we examine this claim in more depth, we must first emphasize the wrong starting point for this evidence. Paul is concerned with how one worships (which was often done in the privacy of their own homes), not with how one appears in public. Having said that, the claim that a married Roman women would often cover her head in public does have some merit. Here are two quotations from respected writers on Roman dress:

> "The palla was a large rectangle of cloth, without the curved lower edge of the toga, that covered the body from shoulder to knee or lower calf . . . it soon became a necessary covering for a modest woman, and no

---

92. Wayne Grudem – *Evangelical Feminism and Biblical Truth* (Wheaton, Illinois: Crossway Books, 2012), 334 (answer 9.2b).
93. Olson, *Dress,* 22.

respectable woman would leave her house without her head covered and her body concealed by it."[94]
Alexandra Croom (*Roman Clothing and Fashion*)

"A married woman's rank, status and morality were also supposed to be indicated by her dress: long tunic, stola, and palla or mantle, drawn over the head when the woman was out of doors, and hair bound with fillets. This description is offered by several modern scholars as that of the everyday clothing of the Roman matron."[95]
Kelly Olson (*Dress and the Roman Woman*)

The problem with this evidence is that it's only half of the story. The other side is told by these very same scholars, but it is not told by Christian theologians advocating the "marriage veil" view. Here are four facts that will portray the other side of the story and help provide a more complete picture of this practice in first century Roman culture.

1. **The literary evidence and archaeology evidence often contradict one another.**
   "There is some disjunction, then, between the literary and the artistic sources for the costume of the Roman woman (and for that of the young girl). Various articles of clothing such as stola and fillets were very strongly linked with the appearance of the honorable married woman in literary sources, yet these 'signs of purity' are by no means ubiquitous in the visual record. . . .
   "Modern authors have stated that the covered head was part of the everyday costume of the Roman matron. But again we must note a disjunction between literary and

---

94. A.T. Croom, *Roman Clothing and Fashion* (Charleston, SC: Tempus Publishing, 2000), 87.
95. Olson, *Dress*, 25.

artistic evidence." [96]

2. Roman women are seen bareheaded in portraits *more often* than with their heads covered.

"The vast majority of female portrait busts we possess show the woman with an unveiled head, probably in order to display her elaborate hairstyle to the viewer." [97]

"Public marble portraits of women at Corinth, presumably members of wealthy and prestigious families, are most frequently shown bare-headed." [98]

"Because most of the women's portraits presented here portray women with uncovered heads, one may infer that bareheadedness in itself was not a sign of a socially disapproved lifestyle." [99]

3. There was not only one "Roman" costume. Roman dress would vary by province, and different provinces had different customs on head covering.

"The provinces of the Roman Empire stretched from Spain to Syria, from Scotland to Egypt, and covered a great many different nations and tribes. The Romans . . . accepted that different people had different cultures and did not attempt to convert them all to an Italian Roman way of life." [100]

4. Corinth was a multi-cultural city and Roman women would often wear their native costume, rather than Roman costume.

"Clothes also helped to identify race or nationality. Native costume was worn, particularly by women, during the first and second century at least, even by those who had a Romanised lifestyle." [101]

---

96. Olson, *Dress*, 34, 40.

97. Olson, *Dress*, 34.

98. Gill, "Roman Portraiture."

99. Thompson, "Hairstyles," 112.

100. Croom, *Roman Clothing*, 123.

101. Croom, *Roman Clothing*, 145.

"It is often the women who retained their native fashions while men adopted Greek or Roman fashions, so that a gravestone can show a woman in native costume and the man in a toga or in a Greek tunic and mantle." [102]

So while married Roman women may have often covered their heads in public (a fact I'm not trying to cast doubt upon), this was *far* from being a unanimous practice. This type of partial observance is not what we would expect, if this was the cultural symbol of being married.

Vestal Virgins

The Vestal Virgins provide us with key evidence that a covered head was not the standard sign of being married in Roman culture. These women were priestesses of Vesta who *"cultivated the sacred fire that was not allowed to go out."* [103] They *"were freed of the usual social obligations to marry and bear children, and took a vow of chastity in order to devote themselves to the study and correct observance of state rituals."* [104] These women were highly respected, and a marriage to a former Vestal (after her thirty years of service) was thought to bring good luck. Alexandra Croom, in *Roman Clothing and Fashion*, writes:

"The Vestal Virgins are the most well-known of Roman priestesses, holding a very special role in Roman public life. . . . The most important elements, as with the bride, was the covering for the head." [105]

These well-known respected women, who took vows of virginity, covered their heads. Clearly, then, the head covering was not a sign that they were married. Nobody in their culture would have interpreted it in that way.

---

102. Croom, *Roman Clothing*, 124.

103. "Vestal Virgin'" Wikipedia, accessed May 30, 2014, https://en.wikipedia.org/wiki/Vestal_Virgin.

104. Ibid.

105. Croom, *Roman Clothing*, 112.

Early Christian Witness

Another relevant piece of evidence is how early Christians understood Paul's command. Tertullian, writing just 150 years after Paul's letter to the Corinthians, knew first-hand what the church in Corinth was still practicing in his day. In one of his books, called *On The Veiling of Virgins*, he said:

"*So, too, did the Corinthians themselves understand him. In fact, at this day the Corinthians do veil their virgins. What the apostles taught, their disciples approve.*"[106]

A question the "marriage veil" advocates need to ask themselves is: *Why would the Corinthian church veil their virgins in AD 200 if they knew it was their culture's symbol of being married?*

Jerome (AD 347–420) also affirms this practice for unmarried women while speaking about "*virgins and widows*" in Egypt and Syria "*who have vowed themselves to God.*" He said that these women do not "*go about with heads uncovered in defiance of the apostle's command, for they wear a close-fitting cap and a veil.*"[107]

So based on an examination of Church history, Roman culture, and the biblical data, I find no reason why this practice should be limited to married women. Let's conclude by briefly talking about how early a girl should start this practice.

What about Young Girls?

The question regarding what age girls should start covering their heads is challenging because it is not answered in Scripture. Since that is the case, I firmly believe the final decision rests with the parents and/or their local church

---

106. Tertullian, "On Veiling of Virgins," 33.
107. Jerome, *Letters*, 292.

(should they have any rules regarding this matter). For myself, since the Bible specifically mentions that it's for "praying and prophesying" I take that as a cue that Paul is speaking about people who can actively participate in worship.

When my girls were babies I didn't cover their heads since they couldn't pray. However, once they could pray along with us, they started covering. For both of my girls this was sometime around age two. I realize that may be earlier than necessary, but no harm is done in that. I look at it as a teaching tool to show them how we are to approach God (Proverbs 22:6), and they feel "grown-up" for participating in something we are doing corporately.

Summary

Paul tells us that we practice head covering "because of the angels" and because it conceals human glory. He does not say that head covering shows that a person is married. Those who hold this view usually arrive at this conclusion from cultural analysis (and as I've argued, an incomplete one) rather than biblical exegesis. Since there are no compelling historical or biblical reasons to see head covering as a sign of marriage, it should be practiced by all women, regardless of their marital status. When a single woman does this she proclaims publicly that she accepts God's order of creation. She affirms that she as a woman has been created to help, not to possess headship. Regarding the age when girls should start covering, the freedom rests in the parents' hands. Having said that, I recommend beginning when children can participate in corporate worship.

SECTION FOUR

CONCLUDING THOUGHTS

CHAPTER FOURTEEN

Will You Symbolize Your Role (Even If No One Else Does)?

"If a woman is invited to the Palace (or even Ascot!) to meet the Queen, she is normally required to wear a hat. Few women refuse the Queen's request, or are ashamed to be seen wearing a hat in these circumstances. Shall we show less respect for the declared wishes of the King of kings?" [108]
Dr. David Gooding, Professor Emeritus of Old Testament Greek at Queen's University, Belfast

To stand alone is hard, really hard. It's tough to go against the grain and be different. There is comfort and safety in numbers. No one wants to be stared at, looked down upon, laughed at, or left out. No one wants to be the crazy, different person. For many women who are convinced head covering is for today, taking the leap to practice it alone is often the scariest part. "If only there were others" is their cry. I want to end this book with an encouragement to serve your sisters in Christ by being one of the "others" and to

---

108. David Gooding, "Symbols of Headship and Glory," *The Word* (Belfast, 1980).

122

join me in helping see this beautiful symbol restored.

The Lone Dancer

I remember watching a TED Talk a few years back about how a movement is started. The speaker played a video of a young man dancing outside by himself. All around him people were relaxing and enjoying the sun, and this guy was making a fool of himself by dancing wildly alone. This lone dancer, the speaker pointed out, is a leader. Shortly after, one other guy joins him in dancing, and they "brave ridicule" together. Then another joins them, and another. Soon a whole crowd of people are dancing like fools together. The speaker points out that "as more people jump in, it's no longer risky." He continues, "They won't stand out; they won't be ridiculed." The crowd felt comfortable because there were so many other people doing it too. They were the majority. However, that wouldn't have been the case without the first brave guy. Someone needed to stand up and start. When that person does so, he makes it easier for others to follow. I want to challenge you to be that person.

Being the First

As I hear testimonies of why women both start and stop covering, it's often connected to what other people are doing at their church.

Desiree Hausam in her testimony shared that what led her to start covering was the fact that a friend of hers *"began to wear a hat in worship."* [109] This led Desiree to restudy the topic with her husband, and, once convinced,

---

109. Desiree Hausam, "Covering Testimony," http://www.headcoveringmovement.com/testimonies/covering-testimony-desiree-hausam, accessed on Oct. 12, 2015.

she began to practice it too. Similarly, Danica Churchill mentioned in her testimony that *"a family began attending our church who came in wearing headcoverings when no one else was practicing it."*[110] That family had to stand alone, but it inspired Danica and her husband to search the Scriptures for themselves. Now not only do the Churchills practice it, but so do many others in their church, including their pastor and his wife.

There are many women in our churches who are convinced head covering is for today, but they are afraid to stand alone. Here's how one lady on the *Head Covering Movement* website described her dilemma:

"It's so hard to find a local person that [practices head covering]. If I were to find someone in [my area] that I could do it with, I would do it more easily. I know I need to, but I won't. It's just so nerve-wracking and I know that's to be expected, but it still makes me not want to—when I know I need to."

This is not to say disobedience to this command is justified because of fear, but I am sympathetic. How great would it would have been if she did not have to stand alone! One person setting the example will by her action encourage others to follow.

Be Like Alice

My hope is that if no one at your church covers (or if very few do), you will determine to be like Alice. Alice said on the *Head Covering Movement* website that she was *"convicted [that head covering should be practiced] a number of years ago but rejected the prompts of [her] conscience for reasons of pride and vanity (not wanting to stick out, fear of what others would think.)."* Alice, understandably, didn't

---

110. Danica Churchill, "Covering Testimony," http://www.headcoveringmovement.com/testimonies/covering-testimony-danica-churchill, accessed Oct. 12, 2015.

want to stand alone. The sad consequence, though, is that she said for *"four years I have struggled spiritually because when I truly searched my heart I found this issue again and was unwilling to revisit it."* When we know what we ought to do and don't, that is sin (James 4:17). Unrepentant sin greatly affects our spiritual growth, as Alice attested. Alice then said, *"I have not yet covered for a worship service, but I will beginning this weekend. I am greatly afraid of attracting attention, but I now understand that my obedience to God is so much more important than any other consideration, and I am going to make this step."*

The person who stands alone is not only a leader but a servant. She serves her fellow sisters by doing a hard thing for them. She bears the ridicule (whether perceived or real) and determines that she will be the one seen as "odd" so her fellow sisters don't have to. By her obedience she makes it easier for other women to follow. Not only that, but as Desiree and Danica can attest, she will cause other people to search the Scriptures for themselves to determine if head covering is true.

So as we close, I want to leave you with one final question: *will you symbolize your role through head covering even if you are alone in doing so?* Ponder the question for a moment and then answer out loud. By practicing this symbol you can have the immense privilege of visually proclaiming God's order of Creation to the church and to the angels. You will be silently portraying the beauty of complementarian roles and playing a vital part in helping to restore this almost forgotten symbol. But, most importantly, you will have peace and joy in knowing that you are walking in obedience to the Lord's command. God's order of Creation is a masterpiece, so let's joyfully display it, as He has decreed.

APPENDICES

Appendix 1
The Head Covering Movement

The *Head Covering Movement* (est. 2013) is a campaign that seeks to spark a return to the practice of head covering during corporate Christian worship. It was founded by the author of this book and can be accessed at headcoveringmovement.com.

On this website you will find articles, testimonies, videos, sermons, and much more. The website is set up to be a resource hub so that you can continue studying this topic and go into more depth than I was able to in this book. You will also find a large community of people there who practice this symbol and comment regularly. I would like to invite you visit the website and become a part of this movement.

To reach the author of this book please visit headcoveringmovement.com/contact. If you have begun to practice this symbol, we would love to hear your story, which you can share at headcoveringmovement.com/share-your-story.

Appendix 2
The Gospel for Head-Covering Christians

There is nothing more important than making sure we understand the gospel properly. Believing and acting upon this message is what saves us, and distorting or refusing to heed this message makes us accursed (Galatians 1:8). It is possible for you to believe in the proper roles of men and women, to practice modesty, and to wear a head covering, and still end up in hell. Why? Because we are not justified[111] by what we do (Ephesians 2:8–9). I would like to share the best news in the world with you now.

God

God is the Creator of all things seen and unseen. He is eternal, perfect, and lacks nothing. He is only one God in being (James 2:19), but three in person (Matthew 28:19). The Father, Son, and Holy Spirit are each a different person of God, but are not three Gods.[112] He has uniquely revealed Himself to us in the Bible, and it is because of this we can know Him.

Creation

God created the first humans, Adam and Eve, and they were in perfect relationship with Him. There was no sin, death, disease, or suffering in the universe. This is the world that God made.

---

111. Justification is a legal proclamation that we are declared "just" or righteous.

112. This teaching is called the Trinity. While the word is not used in the Bible, the concept is taught all throughout it. For more info please read *The Forgotten Trinity* by James White (Bethany House Publishers, 1998).

Fall

God gave Adam and Eve complete freedom with only one prohibition. They were not to eat of the fruit of the *"tree of the knowledge of good and evil"* (Genesis 2:17). The consequences for disobeying God would be both spiritual and physical death. Adam, who is the head of the human race, rebelled against God by eating of that forbidden fruit. They were promptly kicked out of God's presence in the Garden of Eden (spiritual death) and were denied access to the Tree of Life, which would have allowed them to live forever (physical death). Because Adam represented the whole human race, we bear the consequences of his choice (Romans 5:12). His choice was ours too. From that time and continuing today, everyone is born in sin (Psalm 58:3). That means we are born separated from God (Romans 5:10), and our inclination is towards evil and rebellion (Romans 3:10–18). We are hopeless in our state and can do nothing to make ourselves clean before God.

Law

God revealed his holy Law, which was to be obeyed to the letter under the Old Covenant.[113] However, He later clarified that the true purpose of the Law was not to make us right before God but rather to show us our sinfulness (Romans 7:6–7). The Law acts like a mirror so that when we look at it, we see that we don't measure up. Take a quick self-examination from the Ten Commandments. Have you ever stolen anything (irrespective of its value)? Have you ever born false witness (lied)? Have you ever used God's name in vain (used it improperly)? Have you ever dishonored your parents? These commandments may seem to be a small deal, but they are very serious to God. How

---

113. The covenant that God established between Himself and the Israelites.

about the most important commandment of all: have you always loved God with all your heart, soul, mind, and strength?

God has further revealed that He not only judges our actions but our thoughts and intentions too. He will judge those who lust as if they committed adultery (Matthew 5:28). He will judge those who hate as if they had murdered (1 John 3:15). There are heart sins, like greed, selfishness, envy, unforgiveness, and pride. There are also sins of omission, where if we know we are to do something good but we don't do it, we sin (James 4:17). The longer we stare at God's Law, the more condemned we should see ourselves as. We will all give an account to God for every word, thought, and deed on the day of Judgment (Revelation 20:12). The punishment for all who have sinned is eternity in a place called hell. In this place there will be weeping and gnashing of teeth (Matthew 13:41–42).

Rescue

Before the world was formed, God already had a plan to save us (Ephesians 1:4). About two thousand years ago the climax of this plan was revealed in the person of Jesus of Nazareth. He was fully God, having always existed with the Father and the Holy Spirit (John 17:5). However, at this time God entered His own Creation and took on human flesh. He was born into this world through a virgin and became truly human. He never stopped being God but chose to lay aside His divine power during His time on earth (Philippians 2:5–7). He fully relied upon the Holy Spirit for everything. Jesus was the second Adam, the Head of a new people. Unlike the first, Jesus perfectly obeyed the commands of God and lived the sinless life that none of us ever could.

Jesus came here on a mission to secure our redemption, and to accomplish that He also needed to die. Though completely innocent, he was betrayed, mocked, tortured, and executed in the most horrific way. The worst part of all was still yet to come. Every single sin that we have ever committed (past and future) has stored up wrath for us (Romans 2:5). While He hung on the cross, the Father poured out all the wrath that was meant for you and me onto Him (2 Corinthians 5:21). Jesus volunteered to take this upon Himself so that we wouldn't have to bear it. This was the greatest act of love ever demonstrated.

Resurrection

Three days after His death, Jesus was physically raised to life and appeared to over five hundred eyewitnesses (1 Corinthians 15:6). He then ascended to heaven and sat down at the right hand of God, where He rules over the earth as King. He will return again one day to judge the living and the dead (1 Peter 4:5).

Adoption

God offers complete forgiveness of sins as a free gift to anyone in the world. This is apart from any work or deeds that we have done (Galatians 2:16). You can receive this forgiveness today, by putting your faith and trust in Jesus alone to save you. This means you believe the message of the gospel and no longer rely on anything or anyone other than Jesus to save you. God promises that those who do trust Him, receive a second birth (1 Peter 1:23). You are now born into this new race of people whose head is no longer the first Adam but the second (Jesus). His death cancels out the debt we owed God for our sin, and His perfect obedience is credited to our account so that we are seen as righteous before the Father.

We are now adopted into the family of God. An actual miracle has happened in your life where the Holy Spirit comes to dwell inside you and He gives you a brand-new heart with new desires (Ezekiel 11:19–20). You will begin to love the things that He loves (righteousness) and hate the things that he hates (sin). Your faith will be proved genuine by the fruit you bear (Matthew 7:16–20) and your desire to obey His commands (John 14:15). Those who will follow Him are to be baptized and to turn from their sin (Act 2:38).

New Creation

Those who trust in Christ can now eagerly await (rather than dread) the return of King Jesus. He is coming back and has told us that He will make all things new. The world will be restored to its pre-Fall condition, where there will no longer be any pain, sickness, disease, or death (Revelation 21:4). God Himself will dwell among us, and we will get to see His face. We will live together with Him and all other believers forever. Until He returns, we seek to know Him better and to make Him well-known. The glory of God is our passion.

The rest of the story has been written down for us in God's Word, the Bible.[114] I truly hope you do believe this message. If you do, we have unity and you are my brother or my sister. Amen!

---

114. I recommend starting in the New Testament with the Book of Matthew and then reading right through to the end of the Book of Revelation. For an excellent overview of the Bible, watch "The Hope" at www.thehopeproject.com.

Appendix 3
Do I Need to Be Part of a Local Church?

In chapter 12 I made a case for head coverings being a symbol for the gathered local church. However, some think of the local church as an invention of man that finds no basis in Scripture. I would like to make a short case for why the Bible assumes every Christian is an active member of a local church. For clarification's sake, when I say "member" I mean that you are submitting to the pastoral leadership of a specific congregation and have chosen to serve and use your gifts there.

Let's start working through some relevant verses:

> *"And let us consider how to stimulate one another to love and good deeds, not forsaking our own assembling together, as is the habit of some, but encouraging one another; and all the more as you see the day drawing near."* (Hebrews 10:24–25)

We are told from this Scripture to not neglect meeting together with other Christians. We see that one of the main purposes is so we can be a mutual encourager of one another. It is evident from this verse that we are not to be lone rangers; rather we are to be in community. This cannot be fulfilled by listening to or watching sermons at home.

> *"If any man aspires to the office of overseer, it is a fine work he desires to do. An overseer, then, must be . . . one who manages his own household well . . . (but if a man does not know how to manage his own household, how will he take care of the church of God?)"* (1 Timothy 3:1–2, 4–5)

In this passage the office of overseer (pastor/elder) is explained. Paul says that they labor in preaching and teaching (1 Timothy 5:7) and they are to *take care of the church of God.*" This office also involves the exercising of authority, which is why women are forbidden from taking this position (1 Timothy 2:12). The fact that the offices of overseer and deacon (1 Timothy 3:8–13) are established show us that "organized religion" and "local churches" are God's idea.

> *"Obey your leaders and submit to them, for they keep watch over your souls as those who will give an account. Let them do this with joy and not with grief, for this would be unprofitable for you."* (Hebrews 13:17)

In this text we are told to submit to our spiritual leaders (Hebrews 13:7, 24). Every Christian is accountable to a local church, and its pastors are accountable to God for you. Paul said that elders "rule" (1 Timothy 5:17) and "exercise authority" (1 Timothy 2:11), which means they have people under them who are to follow them. Because the leadership will have to give an account, they need to know you. This means committing yourself to a church, rather than church hopping. This also means that if you are in a larger church that you make yourself known to the leadership rather than hiding in the crowd.

> *"Therefore if the whole church assembles together and all speak in tongues, and ungifted men or unbelievers enter, will they not say that you are mad? But if all prophesy, and an unbeliever or an ungifted man enters, he is convicted by all, he is called to account by all."* (1 Corinthians 14:23–24)

Paul here speaks about the the whole church assembling together. He goes on to show that in these meetings there was the exercising of spiritual gifts, teaching, and singing (1

Corinthians 14:26). This was a formal public gathering, as Paul speaks about an unbeliever being able to enter the assembly and take in the worship service. James also references the Christian assembly in his teaching on the sin of judging by appearances (James 2:1–4).

"But to each one is given the manifestation of the Spirit for the common good. . . . since you are zealous of spiritual gifts, seek to abound for the edification of the church." (1 Corinthians 12:7; 14:12)

Every single Christian has been given at least one spiritual gift, and its purpose is to benefit the gathered church. When we neglect church participation, we make God's purpose in spiritual gifts void. We essentially take the gift that He designed to be used for others and bury it. Paul's big theme in 1 Corinthians 14 is using our gifts, with the aim of building up the church.

"If he refuses to listen to them, tell it to the church; and if he refuses to listen even to the church, let him be to you as a Gentile and a tax collector." (Matthew 18:17)

The final step of church discipline is excommunication. So if I had a grievance against you and you didn't listen, where would I bring my grievance if you weren't part of a local church? I would have no way to carry out the Lord's command. Also, Christians are to go to the church instead of suing one another (1 Corinthians 6:4–5). Once again, there is no way to obey that verse unless you are actually a part of and submissive to a local church. Paul speaks about the Corinthians' failure to conduct church discipline on a man in sexual immorality who should *"be removed from among you"* (1 Corinthians 5:2 ESV). There is no way to remove someone from among you unless that person was first a part of you. That is church membership.

Final Thoughts

Being a member of a local church is assumed all throughout the New Testament. Listening to sermons or watching televised services are not a substitute because the purpose of church is not just receiving information. We are called to submit. We are called to serve. We are called to encourage. And we are called to partake of the Lord's Supper (1 Corinthians 11:17–34). It is vital that each of us become members of a local congregation, not allowing anything (including a work schedule) to get in the way of regular fellowship. I am aware that that it can be difficult to find a sound local church, but just remember that there are no perfect churches. Trying to find one with similar beliefs as you (same view of gender roles, baptism, etc.) is good, but don't expect to find a church that understands *everything* the same way you do. You do not have to join a "head covering" church for example. Find a group of saints who love Jesus and preach the gospel, and commit to being a part of them.

Finding a Church

The ministry of 9Marks has done the body of Christ a service in pointing out nine different things that make up a healthy local church. They also have a "church search" section that will help you find a congregation that believes and practices these nine marks. You can visit their website at www.9marks.org or call them at 888-543-1030 for more information. Another great resource is The Gospel Coalition's Church Directory at churches.thegospelcoalition.org.

Printed in Great Britain
by Amazon